William Ouseley

Persian Miscellanies

An essay to facilitate the reading of Persian manuscripts; with engraved specimens,
philological observations, and notes critical and historical.

William Ouseley

Persian Miscellanies
An essay to facilitate the reading of Persian manuscripts; with engraved specimens, philological observations, and notes critical and historical.

ISBN/EAN: 9783337288945

Printed in Europe, USA, Canada, Australia, Japan

Cover: Foto ©Thomas Meinert / pixelio.de

More available books at **www.hansebooks.com**

PERSIAN MISCELLANIES:

AN ESSAY

TO FACILITATE THE READING

OF

PERSIAN MANUSCRIPTS;

WITH ENGRAVED SPECIMENS, PHILOLOGICAL OBSERVATIONS,
AND NOTES CRITICAL AND HISTORICAL.

By *WILLIAM OUSELEY*, E*s*q.

London:

PRINTED FOR RICHARD WHITE,
OPPOSITE BURLINGTON HOUSE, PICCADILLY.

1795.

[Entered at Stationers Hall.]

TO

THE RIGHT HONOURABLE

FRANCIS RAWDON HASTINGS,

EARL OF MOIRA,

BARON RAWDON,

&c. &c.

MY LORD,

WHEN I requested permission to dedicate these pages to your Lordship, it was not merely with the hope that the name of a good and of a great man might save them from perishing with the trifles of the day: It has been the fate of many works, to bear in their Dedications, the high sounding titles of great men, who, from the very nature of their subjects, were incapable of understanding them. But, my Lord, from your knowledge of the Eastern languages,

and

and particularly of the Perfian, this work is addreffed to your Lordfhip with peculiar propriety; and, however inconfiderable, I truft it will be received, as a proof of the very fincere refpect, with which I have the honour to be,

    My Lord,

        Your Lordfhip's obedient

            and humble fervant,

                WILLIAM OUSELEY.

London, Sept. 12, 1795.

INTRODUCTION.

THAT ambition of fame which teaches many to confider as unworthy of attention thofe minuter fubjects from which little reputation for genius can be expected, I had long fuppofed to be the caufe, why, among thofe who have contributed to the advancement of Oriental Literature, fo little has been done on that introductory branch, of which the following Effay principally treats.

But of this neglect, I was induced to feek another caufe, when the fubject of the work which I had undertaken, acquired fome importance, in my own opinion, from the confideration, that, without a previous knowledge of petty matters, it is almoft impoffible to attain a high
degree

degree of eminence in any science; that the theory of musical sounds cannot be perfectly comprehended by him who is unacquainted with the gammut, and that the greatest scholar must have undergone the drudgery of the alphabet.*

And encouraged by the example of so illustrious a critic as Quintilian, who thinks nothing unconnected with the art of Oratory, which is necessary to the formation of an eloquent speaker†, I began to regard as no inconsiderable branch of Eastern literature, the study of the Graphic art, as cultivated among the Persians; without a knowledge of which no man can be pronounced a perfect Orientalist.

And having, by these considerations, given a degree of importance to the subject I was about to undertake, I

---

* "If what appears little, be universally despised, nothing greater can be attained; for all that is great was at first little, and rose to its present bulk by gradual accessions and accumulated labours,"—Johnson's Rambler, No. 83.

† "Sive contemnentes tanquam parva, quæ prius discimus studia," &c.—" Ego cum nihil existimem arti oratoriæ alienum, sine quo oratorem non posse fieri, fatendum est, nec ad ullius rei summam nisi precedentibus initiis pervenire, ad minora illa, sed quæ si negligas, non fit majoribus locus, demittere me non recusabo," &c.—Quintil: Instit: orator: Proem. Lib. i.

naturally

naturally became defirous to know the caufe why others had fo long neglected it; from the evident utility of a work, which might tend to remove the obftacles oppofed to the ftudent on his very firft fetting out, (and which muft be overcome before the object of his purfuit can be attained) it appeared ftrange that no perfon had undertaken the tafk, and I lamented that it was left for one fo infufficiently qualified as myfelf to execute.

But on the commencement of the following work, I difcovered the caufe of this neglect; for the difficulty of arrangement, and the extreme drynefs of the fubject have proved fuch, as, more than once, have nearly forced me to abandon the defign. and muft have deterred from the profecution of it, any perfon not poffeffing a confiderable fhare of patience and perfeverance.

With fcarce any other qualification than thefe, I undertook the work, and have collected in the following pages, and endeavoured to arrange in fome degree of order, the fcattered obfervations I had made during the infancy of my acquaintance with the Perfian language; when, in attempting to decipher Manufcripts, a confiderable portion of time was neceffarily confumed, which fuch a work as I now offer to the public, might, perhaps, have faved.

When we reflect on the difficulties that frequently occur among ourfelves, in reading the familiar letters of our friends: when we confider that many are puzzled in deciphering even what has been written by themfelves, we cannot wonder that more ferious obftacles are prefented to the learner of a new language, and a ftrange character: a character, too, that, from its conftruction, and the facility with which combinations may be formed, allows the writer to indulge in infinite liberties. It is therefore vain to expect that a work of this nature can even approach perfection; no fyftem of rules, however well arranged, being capable of governing the caprices of the Penman.

I am, notwithftanding this, induced to hope, that the following Effay, fuch as it is, may prove of fome fervice to the Perfian fcholar; for fuch an Affiftant I have often wifhed, when ftruggling with the various difficulties that arife from the hurry, negligence, or fancy of tranfcribers: and to the Student, in a fimilar embarraffment, who cannot

not have the advantages of oral inftruction, this work is offered. Clofe application, however, with patience and perfeverance, which, as I before mentioned, are indifpenfably neceffary, will foon render my labours fuperfluous. But, above all, tranfcribing for two or three hours every day, from manufcripts correctly written, will prove of fervice to the learner; and this may be done, even at a time when he is nearly ignorant of the language, and the meaning of feveral words in the original. Such a practice, continued for a few weeks, will infenfibly furnifh the memory with phrafes, which a Dictionary will at leifure explain: Nay, without the affiftance of fuch a work, from analogy, and the frequent recurrence of any particular word in conftruction with others, the learner may frequently afcertain the fenfe of a paffage, and acquire, in the mean time, the moft ufeful habit of reflection. Information, obtained in this manner, by his own induftry, will prove not only more grateful to the Student, but I can venture to affirm, infinitely more profitable than that which he indolently derives from the labours of another. At all events, the practice of frequent tranfcribing from correct originals, will infallibly

fallibly promote the object of this work, by rendering the written character eafy and familiar.

And that the Student muſt be perfectly acquainted with the written character, before he can expect either profit or pleaſure from his Oriental purſuits, is obvious from the conſideration, that the great maſs of Aſiatic Literature (and particularly Perſian) yet remains in manuſcript; to the labours of ſome learned German and Dutch linguiſts, we are principally indebted for many valuable works in Arabic that have iſſued from the preſs; but of Perſian, until the inſtitution of the Aſiatic Society, (from which, much is to be expected) five or ſix compoſitions alone, of any merit, have appeared in print: in Holland, during the laſt century, and recently in England, if we except partial extracts, ſcattered through Dictionaries, Grammars, and works of a ſimilar nature.

Yet, that innumerable treaſures will reward the pains of him, who ſhall explore the mine of Perſian literature, I am well perſuaded, more from the united teſtimonies of others, who have devoted themſelves to the ſtudy of it, than from any ſuperficial knowledge, which I have hitherto been

INTRODUCTION. xi

able to acquire of the Eaſtern languages; but by thoſe unacquainted with the literature of Aſia, the praiſes which Orientaliſts beſtow on the writers of that country, are aſcribed, leſs to their intrinſic merits, than to the partial enthuſiaſm of a commentator, employed on a favorite ſubject: as thoſe who poſſeſs no muſic in their ſouls, and are dead to all the powers of harmony, can read without emotion, and are unable to comprehend the moſt animated, or deſcriptive paſſages of a Rouſſeau, or a Burney.

On the characters uſed by the ancient Perſians, I have not, in this Eſſay, offered any obſervations, referving that branch of Oriental Antiquities, for the ſubject of inveſtigation in a future work*. Neither have I enquired into the probable nature of thoſe learned writings, which, as *Nizamì* aſſures us, in his Hiſtory of Alexander the Great, were tranſlated, after the conqueſt of Perſia, into the native language of the Victorious Prince. They have, it is to be feared, periſhed in the ſame tide of Time, which has

* Alphabets of the *Pehlevi* and *Zend*, are given in that admirable work, " De Fatis " Linguarum Orientalium Commentatio," Vienna, 1780, Folio.

effaced

effaced the ancient *painting*, celebrated by the Perfian poet ; whether the tranflations have efcaped thofe conflagrations fo fatal to Grecian literature, and ftill moulder in an obfcure corner of the Byfantine, or of fome Monaftic Library, would be no unworthy object of curious inquiry. Although I have ftudied, in the following pages, to reprefs a natural tendency to the inveftigation of antiquities, and have referved much for future difcuffion, yet I muft here anticipate a remark, which many of my readers will probably make, that, " of the notes and obfervations fcattered " through this work, the greater number inclines to that " favourite fubject;" in excufe, I plead the very interefting nature of that country's antiquities, whofe language, and modern character, I have principally treated of; that country, to whofe ancient monarchs, all the princes of the known world bowed the head*, while they " reigned " from India, even unto Ethiopia, over an hundred, and

---

* " Thus faith Cyrus, king of Perfia, The Lord GOD of Heaven, hath given me " all the kingdoms of the Earth, &c." Ezra Chap. I. v. 2.

" feven

INTRODUCTION.

"seven and twenty provinces*: sitting in Imperial state, on splendid thrones, adorned with all the

> "Wealth of Ormus and of Ind,
> "Or where the gorgeous East with richest hand,
> "Showers on her kings, Barbaric pearls and gold†."

OF those Persian monarchs, the gilded palaces, situated in the various quarters of their wide extended dominions, realized, in magnificence and beauty, all that we can conceive of Asiatic splendor, or of edifices raised by magic power, dazzling the eyes of mortal gazers; but of those palaces, the majestic ruins yet to be seen, while they remain a venerable record of the nation's former greatness, afford ample subject for melancholy reflexions, on the decay of empires,

---

* Esther, Chap. I. verse 1.

† Milton's Paradise Lost, Book II. To this Eastern splendor, the poet Spenser also alludes, in his Faery Queen, Book III. Canto 4.
"The Wealth of th' East, and pomp of Persian kings."

INTRODUCTION.

and the revolutions effected by time: for now, to use the words of a Persian poet* :

" The spider holds the veil in the palace of Cæsar,
" The owl stands centinel on the watch-tower of Afrasiab."

AND to the mildness of a happy climate alone, we are probably indebted for the preservation of those sculptured figures, and mysterious inscriptions, that still decorate the walls of the royal apartments, where the victorious Alexander celebrated his triumph over the fallen Darius, and in which the lovely Thais, by the side of the Grecian hero, " sat like a blooming Eastern bride,"—and, but too successfully, urged him to destroy, in one fatal hour of amorous intoxication, the metropolis of the Persian empire, and of the world, with one of the noblest

---

* " Pordeh-darce mikend der kufar-i- keyfar ankiboot,
" Boomy nubet mizend ber kumbed i-Afraslaub."
See the original Persian, in Jones's Grammar, p. 104.

In thefe words, and they were happily applied, did the triumphant Turk, Mahomet II. exclaim, when, having given a final blow to the Roman Empire, in 1453, by the taking of Conflantinople, (where the Greek Emperor fell) he contemplated the Royal Palace of his vanquished fee, which prefented to his view a dreary fcene of havoc and defolation.

productions

INTRODUCTION. xv

productions of human labour and ingenuity—the magnificent palace of the Sons of Cyrus*.

YET, however confiderable may be its majeftic remains, ftill to be feen above ground, it is moft probable that, within the precincts of the ruined palace, treafures, much more precious in the antiquary's eftimation, from long concealment, lie buried in the duft of more than twenty ages. To drag thefe into open day, from the dark receffes

---

* The city of Perfepolis, which covered the extenfive plain of *Chehelminar*, muft have foon yielded to the conflagration, and become an eafy prey to the flames, the houfes (which were probably but flight fabricks) being principally conftructed of cedar and cyprefs wood: But the Palace, fituated on a rifing ground, about 400 paces from the city, was compofed of fuch excellent materials, and conftructed with fuch admirable fkill, that a great part of it fuccefsfully oppofed the progrefs of the fire, and has refifted the affaults of above 2000 years. In the beginning of the prefent century, Monf. Le Bruyn, publifhed engravings of feveral hundred figures cut in relief, which yet remained upon the walls; leaving for future vifitors to copy, fuch a prodigious number of fculptures, that, according to fome travellers (Herbert, Mandelflo, &c.). it would require no common degree of induftry in an able artift to make drawings of them all in the fpace of feveral months. When vifited in 1627 by Sir Thos. Herbert, not only the images cut in marble remained in perfect prefervation, but even the gilding on the walls, and on the drapery of fome figures, retained its original luftre. Time, however, gradually finks many valuable fragments deeper in the earth; and others, from the daily dilapidations of the peafants, may be found in the humble walls of the neighbouring cottages.

of oblivion, is a fpecies of enjoyment for which the princes of the Eaft, who poffefs the power of indulging it, feel not the inclination; and is, I fear, a degree of luxury far beyond the reach or privileges of a folitary European traveller!

AND that valuable and moft curious fubterranean fragments ftill exift at Perfepolis, is an opinion which I have adopted, not merely from the probability that fimilar treafures lie hidden among all vifible ruins of confiderable antiquity, but from the pofitive teftimonies, and ftrong conjectures of feveral ingenious travellers*. Of the figures

at

---

* I have been affured by the Chevalier Clergeau de la Barre, that among the ruins of Babylon and Perfepolis, moft curious and valuable antiques are daily difcovered, many of which are depofited in the cabinets of the European Confuls, refident in the vicinity of thofe places. This ingenious Frenchman, whom I had the pleafure of meeting in Holland, foon after his return from the Eaft, (in the various countries of which he had travelled for twelve years) has hitherto been prevented by domeftic misfortunes, and the civil calamities of his country, from offering to the public, his admirable collection of drawings, taken from the moft venerable monuments of antiquity in India, Perfia, Arabia, and the Levant. In the defarts of Arabia, he difcovered and afcertained the fituation of a fine and very ancient temple, not marked in any map, nor defcribed by any traveller; but on

removing

INTRODUCTION. xvii

at the monument of Ruſtam, (in the vicinity of Perſepolis) ſuppoſed to repreſent that celebrated warrior and his favourite miſtreſs,* the lower parts are concealed in heaps of ſtones and accumulated rubbiſh, which hide perhaps, at the ſame time, ſome ancient inſcriptions, or other intereſting ſculptures. And on that ſpot, not far from the royal palace, where, in the opinion of Sir Tho. Herbert, the famous temple of Diana ſtood, nothing ſtrikes the view but continued piles of earth, " wherein, (to uſe the words " of that well-informed writer) doubtleſs, are buried many " rare pieces of art†."

removing ſome earth which concealed part of a curious ſculpture, one of his guides happening to diſcover the body of a camel not long dead, the others became apprehenſive that the wandering Arabs were at hand, and immediately departed. Among the antiques found at Babylon and Perſepolis, the moſt curious, according to the Chevalier, were ſeveral volumes of parchment, covered with characters hitherto undeciphered, and an emerald of two inches long, containing the figure of Alexander, engraved with ſuch exquiſite art as to be only diſcernible when placed in a particular point of view between the eye and the light.

* See the 5th chapter of this work, p. 97, 114, &c. and the engraving of thoſe figures in Le Bruyn's Travels.

† Herbert's Travels, p. 155.

FROM

INTRODUCTION.

From the jealoufy and fufpicious ignorance of the vulgar in almoſt every country, ſtrangers find confiderable difficulty in examining with attention, any celebrated ruins; but the Perfians, naturally of a romantic turn, vain of their nation's former fplendor, and the ſtriking memorials of it which yet remain, and delighting in thofe traditions which record the deeds of other days, oppofe no obſtacles to the curious traveller, in the inveſtigation of their antiquities; and lefs rigid than the Mahometans of Arabia, they freely permit him to employ his pencil, fo neceffary a companion to the accompliſhed antiquary*.

And from the ſtudy of thofe noble ruins abovementioned, and of the fculptures which they ſtill exhibit, and by a careful comparifon of the ſtatues in the royal Maufolea, fituated in the impending hills, and other ancient monu-

---

* Thus Monf. Le Bruyn, an ingenious painter, who vifited Perfepolis in 1705, was permitted not only to pafs three months in uninterrupted leifure among its venerable remains, and to make drawings of every thing that appeared to him either curious or picturefque, but alfo to employ a ſtone cutter of Shiràz, (a city 30 miles diſtant) to feparate from the mafs of marble fome ancient figures in relief, which he afterwards brought to Europe.

ments,

INTRODUCTION. xix

ments, with the oral and written traditions of the country concerning them, much may yet be done to illuftrate the antiquities of Perfia, which it is my fixed intention, if life and health be fpared, perfonally to explore.

OF the ancient poetry of Perfia, fo fcanty are the Specimens which have defcended to our days, that the induftry of many, who made it the object of their refearch, feems to have been employed in vain : to afcertain therefore, what it may have been, muft be the refult of inveftigation more fuccefsful. The learned Prefident of the Afiatic Society could difcover but a few lines of the ancient *Pahlavi** ; and the ingenious Biographer of the Perfian Poets, could trace them little farther than the time of the Arabian conqueft†. Yet, the climate of the country, the manners, and very nature of men, muft have undergone a total change, or we

---

* Sir William Jones's Anniverfary Differtation on the Perfians, 1789.

† Captain William Kirkpatrick's Introduction to the Hiftory of the Perfian Poets, Afiatic Mifcellany, No. 1.

muft

muſt conclude, that ancient Perſia could boaſt of its poetical productions; its modern inhabitants being a race, which may be ſaid to liſp in numbers; among whom, the cultivation of their language is an important care, and who believe of Poetry, as the ancient Greeks did of Muſic, that it poſſeſſes a faſcinating power, and thence they have ſtyled it, "Lawful Magic."

It will therefore be found, that there is ſcarce any ſpecies of compoſition, which the Perſian poets have not cultivated with ſucceſs, from the didactic or Moral Sentence, to the finiſhed Epic or Heroic Poem: through every gradation of Bacchanalian Ode, Elegiac, and Amorous Sonnet, Allegories amuſing or inſtructive, and Romances founded on hiſtory, or fable: compoſitions breathing all the warmth of a luxuriant ſoil, and decorated with every adventitious grace, that the moſt flowery language can beſtow.

And in this reſpect the Perſians are peculiarly fortunate, their native tongue, from the ſimplicity of its conſtruction, and facility in verſification, being, like the Italian among us, moſt happily adapted to all the purpoſes of poetry, particularly

larly that of the Erotic kind, which feems to be naturally the favourite of the tender and voluptuous Perfian*.

A VERY ſtriking fimilarity of fentiment and imagery may be difcovered in the works of the Italian and Perfian poets ; I ſhall not here dwell on this refemblance which has been pointed out by others. The Sonnets of Petrarch have been compared with thofe of Sàdi : nay, a general fimilarity of manners and cuſtoms has been remarked by one, who, an Italian by birth, was rendered capable, by a long refi-

---

* A learned Orientalift has moft happily defcribed the genius of Perfian Literature by the epithets " foft and elegant." " Jacent, quod vehementer dolco, literæ Perficæ, " *molles* illæet *elegantes*, quarum addifcendarum tu me tanta cupiditate incendifti, ut quid- " quid evenerit, fi modo vivam et valeam, certum fit deliberatumque, raro apud nos ex- " emplo, totum me illis tradere."

See the letter of Profeffor Schultens, to Sir William Jones, written in 1777, quoted in the Dutch Eulogium, or, " Lofreden op Henrik Albert Schultens," by Jacobus Kante- laar. Amſterdam, 1794. Octavo, 77.

And if the ſtudy of poetry, according to a moft excellent critic, is ufeful, " *quod fit jucunda*," the poetical compofitions of Perfia, may boaſt of a peculiar degree of utility : " Poeticam igitur eo præcipue utilem effe ftatuo, quod fit jucunda ;" Lowth's Prælectiones, " de Sacra Poefi Hebræorum ;" Præl. I. vol. I. p. 6, I quote that edition of this admirable work, publifhed at Gottingen, in two volumes, Octavo, 1758, 1761, with the notes and com- ments of the moft learned Michaelis. Of this edition, it is to be remarked, that in the pre- face to the fecond volume, is an addrefs to the venerable author, whom, in the firſt volume, his commentator had, through mifinformation, fpoken of as deceafed.

xxii   INTRODUCTION.

dence in Perfia, of judging with accuracy. The famous traveller, Pietro della Valle, writing from that country near two centuries ago, thus mentions his Perfian friends*, "Ufing " always to me the greateft compliments, and moft cour- " teous fpeeches, &c. in which, and in *all other cuftoms* (for " I have remarked, and fhall, perhaps fome day, commit " them to paper as a curiofity, drawing a parallel in infi- " nite refpects) it appears to me, that the Perfians, refemble " very ftrongly, the people of Naples," &c. and this ingenious author, in many other parts of his work, takes notice of this refemblance; but I have as yet fought in vain, and, indeed, am ftill ignorant, whether he ever fulfilled his defign of publifhing, the parallel mentioned in the above quotation.

BETWEEN many paffages in the Greek and Perfian Poets, a refemblance alfo has been found. We are to confider, that the climate of Greece, furnifhes in many in-

---

* Viaggi di Pietro della Valle, 204.   " Ufando mi fempre grandiffimi complimenti
" e parole molto cortefe, &c. nelli quali, et in ogni altri coftume (che l'ho notate e forfe un
" giorno le fcriverò per curiofita, facendone paralello in infinite cofe) pare a me che i Per-
" fiani fi affomiglino molto alle genti di Napoli."

ftances,

INTRODUCTION. xxiii

ſtances, the ſame ſubjects for glowing and flowery deſcription with that of Aſia; and that many of the Greek Lyric Poets were, by birth, Aſiatics: from which circumſtance, and from the ſimilarity of ſubject and imagery, uſed in their poems, the moſt learned Orientaliſt of the preſent age, ſcarcely ſcruples, in his Latin Commentaries, to claſs them among the Poets of Aſia*: and, it ſhall be my object, in a future work, to demonſtrate, that Homer and Anacreon, unequalled as they are, might not bluſh to have produced the Heroic Poem of Firdauſi, or the Lyric Odes of Hafez. To deny pre-eminence to thoſe claſſics, would beſpeak a taſte as corrupt, and a judgment equally prejudiced, as thoſe of the Grammarian, who quaintly aſſerts, that in compariſon with a particular branch of Oriental Literature, "*the Graces of the Greeks and Romans are graceleſs*†." I ſhall here diſmiſs the ſubject

---

* "Haud ſcio an multi è poetis Græcis, &c. Sir William Jones's "Poeſeos Aſiaticæ Commentarii, p. 16, Octavo, London, 1774. Of this admirable work, another Octavo Edition, appeared in 1777, publiſhed at Leipſig, with the notes of the learned Eichorn."

† "Linguæ ſuavitatem et elegantiam, cum qua collatæ, χαριτες Græcorum ἀχαριτες, et ingratæ Latinorum Gratiæ, &c."

Waſmuth's Arab. Grammar, Parænifis, p. 1.

xxiv INTRODUCTION.

of Perſian Poetry, and return to the principal object of the following Eſſay.

It was, at firſt, my deſign to give only a few engraved ſpecimens from original manuſcripts, and to annex explanations of the chief difficulties that might occur to the ſtudent, from the confuſion or omiſſion of the diacritical points, and the whimſical combination of characters; but I have enlarged my plan, by ſubjoining to the engraved ſpecimens a more minute analyſis, and by prefixing a few general obſervations on each letter of the alphabet, and the diacritical points.

The extracts from the Perſian writers have not been taken at random: although my chief object has been, to familiariſe the learner's eye to the various combinations and contractions of letters, yet in ſo doing, I have been careful to ſelect, in general, ſuch paſſages (and particularly from the Poets) as, to uſe the words of Sir Wm. Jones, on a ſimilar occaſion,* " will give ſome variety to a ſubject

---

* Perſian Grammar, p. 21.

" naturally

INTRODUCTION. xxv

" naturally barren and unpleafant; will ferve as a fpecimen
" of the Oriental ftyle : and will be more eafily retained in
" the memory, than rules delivered in mere profe."

I have likewife ftudied originality in my extracts from the Perfian writers, and it will be found, that (except two or three which I have acknowledged in their places) none have before appeared in print; indeed, as all the manufcripts quoted in this work are in my own poffeffion, I cannot have any reafonable excufe for borrowing from the tranflations of another.

If, in fome few inftances, my tranflations of the Perfian verfes, have not been exactly literal, the Vocabulary at the end of this work, will enable the reader to afcertain the true meaning of the originals; by confulting it he will difcover that, whatever liberties I may have taken with the words, I have never departed from the fenfe of the author: and he will convince himfelf of the impoffibility of transferring, without grofs barbarifms, the idioms of one language into another. The Vocabulary will befides fupply, in fome meafure, the place of a Perfian Dictionary,—a

work,

work, which, from its great utility, and the inceſſant demands of the India market, has become ſcarce and conſequently expenſive; and which cannot, from its bulk, be always conveniently at hand.*

To render the plan of this Eſſay as clear as the complicated nature of its ſubject would admit, I have ſubjoined an explanatory Index, by the aſſiſtance of which, the reader may at once decipher any particular figure given in the firſt four plates, and immediately find the page or pages wherein a reference is made to thoſe figures, and their graphical difficulties diſcuſſed and explained. To avoid re-

---

* Until the indefatigable induſtry of Mr Richardſon furniſhed us with his admirable Dictionary of the Arabic and Perſian languages, in two folio volumes, the only works of that nature which the ſtudent of the latter could reſort to, were the great Onomaſticon of *Meninſki*, and the Lexicon by *Caſtellus*. The former conſiſting of ſeveral volumes, was always inconvenient from its bulk, conſtructed rather for the uſe of the Turkiſh than of the Arabic or Perſian ſcholar: and from its exorbitant price (which once roſe at Calcutta to an hundred guineas) was beyond the reach of moſt young Orientaliſts, until the publication of Mr Richardſon's Dictionary rendered it leſs valuable. The Lexicon compiled by Caſtellus, from the papers of the learned Golius, was publiſhed with all their errors, in a confuſed and inelegant type. As for the Gazo-phylacium of Father Angelo, however curious in many reſpects, it is little more than a defective and inaccurate Vocabulary.

petition,

petition, I have been under the neceffity of frequently referring the reader from one part to another of this work, which in a great meafure, confifts of detached and mifcellaneous effays.

On the fubject of pronunciation I have generally followed the moft approved and correct Englifh writers, in the manner of expreffing by our characters, the founds of Arabic and Perfian words*. In attempting to do this with precifion, a combination of letters is often neceffary, which, to an Englifh eye, appears moft harfh and uncouth; but this is found to be equally the cafe, when the words of any other languages are written by a Foreigner, exactly according to his fyftem of pronunciation. Our own language will not bear the teft: Let us fuppofe a Frenchman to have caught the founds of a few Englifh words, and relying on his ear alone, to have committed them to paper: who would recognize in the

---

* " Of founds, in general, it may be obferved, that words are unable to defcribe them."
—Dr Johnfon's Englifh Grammar.

following

following combination of letters, one of the fweeteft lines of Dryden's Poetry?

"*Chi fird no dain-dgere, farchi nous no ciunc* *.*"

OR what Italian would believe that any line of Petrarch could be fo disfigured, even by the Englifh mode of expreffing founds, as to wear the following harfh appearance, when written according to the powers afcribed by us to the vowels and other letters?

"*Say kol tchec-ako defeer kub'l core diftroojay* †."

YET by this mode of writing, which exhibits as harfh or ridiculous, the fofteft lines of European Poetry have we been obliged to exprefs the founds of Afiatic words ‡. On the fubject of the general orthography of the Eaftern languages, I refer the reader to an elaborate and moft ingenious Effay by Sir William Jones.

AND

---

* She fear'd no danger for fhe knew no fin.—" The Hind and the Panther."
† *Se col cieco defir che'l cor diftrugge.*—" Sonnet xliii. Part I."
‡ From the various powers affigned to letters by different nations, the fame Oriental word, when written by a Frenchman, Italian, Spaniard, &c. affumes a variety of appearances; thus the common Perfian word which we (exactly following the original) write *Chun,*

INTRODUCTION.

AND, I shall close this preface, by deprecating the criticism of those, who having learned from living instructors, the rudiments of Asiatic penmanship, and the technical terms of that art, may smile at the phrases I have adopted, in describing the combinations or forms of letters, since all writers on the subject have used the same, when they studied perspicuity, without circumlocution, as I have proved by some quotations in the second Chapter. Nor let the veteran Orientalist, condemn this Essay, merely because he no longer wants the assistance of such a work; the obstacles which he has surmounted, still lie in the way of others; some have attained their journey's end, but many setting out, still want a guide; should we, because landed on the wished-for shore, despise the pilot, who may yet steer others into port?

Chun, would be spelt *Tchun*, by the French, *Ciun*, by the Italians, &c. and the word *Shah*, which we write according to the Persian orthography, would be *Chah*, in French writings, *Sciah*, among the Italians, *Sjbah*, by Dutch, and *Sah*, by German writers, and has been written *Xa*, by Spanish travellers. I believe it will be found, that the English can best express the sounds, yet nearest approach, in general, the Persian orthography, in respect to consonants and diphthongs; but that, the Italian can best retain the broad accent of the Eastern vowel sounds.

INTRODUCTION.

In the following pages, it has been my only view to render them intelligible to the European ſtudent, who is to derive his knowledge from books alone, and to afford him that aſſiſtance, for which I often wiſhed myſelf : for him, I have undertaken the humble, though laborious taſk of Literary Pioneer, and have endeavoured to remove, in ſome meaſure, the thorns and brambles that oppoſed his entrance to the ſmiling garden of Perſian Literature ; a garden which I would deſcribe, were I allowed to conclude in the Eaſtern ſtyle*, as a happy ſpot, where laviſh nature, with wild profuſion, ſtrews the moſt fragrant and blooming flowers, (1) where the moſt delicious fruits abound, and which is ever vocal, with the plaintive melody of the Nightingale, (2) who, day and night, there, " tunes " her love-laboured ſong :" where aërial beings in a viſionary train, (3) the faireſt creatures of poetical imagination,

---

* The reader will at once perceive, that in this concluding paragraph, I have endeavoured to compriſe the moſt ſtriking features, and frequent ſubjects of Perſian Literature. The praiſes of the roſe, and jeſſamine, and other fragrant flowers, (1) are perhaps too much, the Poet's favourite theme. The *Bulbul* (2) is the almoſt inſeparable companion of the roſe, and the beautiful Perſian Peries, (3) are a ſpecies of imaginary beings, who live on perfumes alone, the exquiſite purity of their nature, rejecting all groſſer nouriſhment.

INTRODUCTION.   xxxi

tion, hover in the balmy clouds, inhaling the odours of the jeffamine and rofe; a garden, in whofe trim alcoves, the feftive board is fpread, and the praifes of ruby wine, (4) fung to the fprightly lyre, while lovely nymphs, with difhevelled mufky treffes, prefent the flowing goblet to the enamoured gueft: (5) a garden, in whofe fhady bowers, and foft receffes, the tender tale of love (6) is ever told, and the fond figh, attuned to the querulous lute, (7) or breathed to the paffing gale; (8) whilft in its more open walks,

Beauty is one of their effential characteriftics; and I am perfuaded, that the name of thofe gentle creatures (like many other words in the Perfian language) is of Hebrew or Chaldaic origin, without any intervention of Arabic, and that its proper root is נצב.

(4) (5) (6). The praifes of love and wine, and the delights of Spring, are, among the Perfians, as with the Greeks of old, the chief fubjects of the Lyric Song: nor do thefe feem lefs enamoured of the Rofe and Nightingale, than the modern Afiatics. Anacreon calls that lovely flower, "the moft excellent of the fragrant tribe; the chief " care of Spring, and the delight even of the Gods." Ode V.

" Ῥόδον ἀφέριστον ἄνθος,
" Ῥόδος ἔαρος μέλημα,
" Ῥόδα καὶ θεοῖσι τερπνά."

And Theocritus prefers " the melody of the Nightingale to the notes of all other birds that wing the air."—Idyll. XII.

——————— " ἔσσιν ἀηδὼν
" Συμπάντων λιγύφωνος ἀοιδοτάτη πετεινῶν."

Of the Perfian Mufic (7), the *Nifeem Seba* (8), or gentle breeze; the *Shah Namah,*
d 2   *Skander*

xxxii   INTRODUCTION.

walks, the high heroic deeds of ancient warriors and kings, (9) are chaunted in lofty ftrains; Science gives her leffon, and the voice of Wifdom is often heard uttering the moral fentence, (10) or delivering the dictates of experience, in the flowery or myfterious phrafe of allegory (11). In fhort, to conclude the metaphor, an ample field of intellectual enjoyment, which requires but a little cultivation to prove itfelf a grateful foil.

Skander Namah, and other Romances (9) and Heroic Poems, I fhall fpeak in the courfe of this work: and whofoever fhall perufe the *Pend Namah* (10), the *Guliſtan* and *Boſtân* (11), of the moral *Sadi*, and many other fimilar productions, muft acknowledge the truth of what I have before afferted, "that there is fcarce any fpecies of compofition which the Perfians have not cultivated with fuccefs."

I NOW haften to prefent this Compilation to the reader, confcious, that, although my defign of affording fome inftruction and entertainment, may have failed, nothing at leaft, has been wilfully inferted, by which the tafte or judgment might be vitiated or mifled, truth or delicacy violated, or morality offended.

INDEX

INDEX

TO THE PAGES WHICH EXPLAIN THE FIGURES IN THE FIRST
FOUR PLATES.

PLATE I.

NO.
1 *AUNCHUNAUN*, (anchnan) page 11
2 *Seraunjaum*, (Sranjam) 11, 16, 30, 35, 36
3 *Aunchek*, (Anch) 11, 36, 39, 50
4 *Aſt*, or *Eſt*, (Aſt) 11, 29, 48
5 *Iſtikbaul*, (Aſtkbal) 11, 32
6 *Daſhtnu*, (Daſhtn) 11, 13, 36
7 *Gulra*, (Glra) 12, 33
8 *Bokhàra*, (Bkhara) 12, 13, 49
9 *Aumedeſt*, (Amdaſt) 12, 56
10 *Firaukh*, (Frakh) 12
11 *Shimſhad*, (Shmſhad) 12, 47, 55
12 *Aumeedùm*, (Amydm) 35, 40
13 *Padiſhah*, (Badſhah) 13, 39
14 *Buſiaur*, (Bſyar) 13, 40

NO.
15 *Pechegaun*, (Pchgan) 13, 36, 16, 33
16 *Becheſhmhay*, (Bchſhmhay) 13, 41, 16, 28, 35, 38
17 *Auftàb*, (Aftab) 14, 47
18 *Aſip*, (Aſp) 14, 47
19 *Teſtym*, (Tſtym) 14, 40
20 *Geety*, (Gyty) 14, 41, 50
21 *Goorifty*, (Grfty) 15, 49, 50
22 *Auftadeh*, (Aftadh) 15, 47
23 *Hedy's*, (Hhdy's) 15, 16, 23
24 *Cheſhim*, (Chſhm) 16, 35
25 *Chèh*, (Chh) 16, 39
26 *Shuky*, (Shuky) 40
27 *Zeleekha*, (Zlykha) 16, 21, 50
28 *Sekhun*, (Skhn) 16, 22, 29
29 *Der*, (Dr) 22

INDEX.

NO.
30 *Dujet*, (Dufl) 22, 28
31 *Rud*, (Rud) 22
32 *Sikander*, (Skndr) 23
33 *Neſhayed*, (Nſhayd) 23, 29, 36
34 *Zoormend*, (Zurmnd) 23
35 *Mandeh*, (Mandh) 23, 39
36 *Chehreh*, (Chhrh) 39

PLATE II.

37 *Anduh*, (Anduh) 39
38 *Hind*, (Hnd) 23, 38
39 *Shud, Sheh*, (Shh) 24, 45, 26, 39
40 *Izaur*, (Æzar) 24, 31
41 *Murd*, (Mrd) 35
42 *Beher*, (Bhr) 25, 38
43 *Zeradhuſht*, (Zrdhſht) 25, 37, 29
44 *Ghemzeh*, (Ghmzh) 25, 31, 35, 39
45 *Seyah*, (Syh) 26, 39
46 *Gulſhen*, (Glſhn) 26, 29
47 *Solyman*, (Slyman) 26, 35, 36, 40
48 *Sádi*, (Sædy) 26, 41, 50, 53, 56
49 *Shirauz*, (Shyraz) 26, 40.
50 *Laſhkur-eſh*, (Lſhkrſh) 28, 56, 63
51 *Khooſheſt*, (Khuſhſt) 28
52 *Imſheb* (Amſhb) 29, 47, 50
53 *Sekhun*, (Skhn) 29, 36

NO.
54 *Peſy*, (Bſy) 30, 41,
55 *Nejret*, (Nſrt) 30
56 *Sehra*, (Shra) 30
57 *Hezret*, (Hhzrt) 30, 50, 56
58 *Tuxk*, (Tuk) 31, 32
59 *Yſhk*, (Æſhk) 49
60 *Ghemm*, (Ghm) 36
61 *Nughmet*, (Nghmt) 31, 32
62 *Guft*, (Gft) 32, 33, 47
63 *Hekyket*, (Hhkyt) 32, 49
64 *Aſhufteh*, (Aſhſth) 32, 39
65 *Firmooden*, (Frmudn) 32, 50
66 *Meſhryk*, (Mſhrk) 30, 32
67 *Leiken*, (Lykn) 33, 37
68 *Yeky*, (Yky) 33, 34
69 *Gumar*, (Gmar) 33
70 *Kemannet*, (Kmant) 33, 49
71 *Gohurhay*, (Ghrhay) 25, 33, 37, 38, 40
72 *Keh*, (Kh) 34, 39

PLATE III.

73 *Hemchunaunk*, (Hmchnank) 34, 38
74 *Goorift*, (Grft) 34, 63
75 *Laſhkur*, (Lſhkr) 34
76 *Jemauleſh*, (Jmalſh) 34
77 *Wallah*, (Wallh) 34, 39
78 *Hemeh*, (Hmh) 35, 38, 39
79 *Men*, (Mn) 36
80 *Chun Men*, (Chun Mn) 36, 64

INDEX.

NO.
81 *Nifeem*, (Nſym) 36
82 *Damen*, (Damn) 36
83 *Mahv*, (Mahy) 37, 45
84 *Mihr*, (Mhr) 38
85 *Hemchu*, (Hmchu) 38, 54
86 *Heyhat*, (Hyhat) 39, 48
87 *Seemeen*, (Symyn) 40, 48
88 *Sawky*, (Saky) 41, 48
89 *Sàdy*, (Sædy) 41
90 *Peri-rooee*, (Pryruy) 41, 47
91 *Gulaùb*, (Glab) 42, 59
92 *Laleh*, (Lalh) 42
93 *Aun aftaubeſt*, (An aftabſt) 45, 56
94 An Equivocal Figure, ſee page 46
95 *Nutwan*, (Ntuan) 47
96 *Kheyal*, (Khyal) 62
97 *Biya*, (Bya) 47
98 *Peer*, (Byr) 47
99 *Picheed*, (Bychd) 48
100 *Keſhteh*, (Kſhth) 48
101 *Shud*, (Shd) 48
102 *Chun*, (Chun) 16, 48
103 *Az Audiſheh Dileſh*, (Zandyſhh Dlſh) 29, 34, 39, 50, 62
104 *Aunkeh*, (Ankh) 50, 53
105 *Bauzy*, (Bazy) 51, 53
106 *Khauk*, (Khak) 51

NO.
107 *Deſt-a-Sàdi*, (Dſt Sædy) 51, 68
108 *Javauby*, (Juaby) 51

PLATE IV.

109 *Daughy* (Daghy) 48, 51
110 *Many*, (Many) 51
111 *Hafyl*, (Hhaſl) 53
112 *Dilfereeb*, (Dlfryb) 53
113 *Kaf*, (Kaf) 53
114 *Hekayety*, (Hhkayty) 54
115 *Heech*, (Hych) 55
116 *Muheyia*, (Mhya) 55
117 *Ghemm'a Yſhk*, (Ghmæſhk) 55
118 *Geſhty Noah*, (Kſhtynuhh) 34, 56
119 *Shudy Gunge*, (Shdyknj) 56
120 *Kaſhgy*, (Kaſhky) 59
121 *Dilruba*, (Dlruba) 59, 63
122 *Porkurdeh az aub*, (Prkrdh az ab) 60
123 *Herkes Sheneedy*, (Hrks Shnydy) 60
124 *Jaume Shraub*, (JamShrab) 61
125 *Dil-dar*, (Dldar) 61
126 *Beeroon Keſhty*, (Byrun Kſhty) 61
127 *Der een Wekt*, (Drynukt) 61
128 *Aunzemeen*, (Anzymn) 62
129 *Ger Kurd, Mugur Keh*, (Gr Krd, Mgr Kh) 62

INDEX.

NO.		NO.	
130	*Az Amber Serishtch*, (Az Ænbr Srshth) 62		(Aura Dur Aurd Az Du-Rud) 64
131	*Sh-Nakhash*, (Sh-Nksh) 63	137	*Gulzar-e-Irem*, (Glzar Arm) 65, 67
132	*Nedeedeh*, (Ndydh) 63		
133	*Bergrift*, (Brgrft) 63	138	*Buzruk Gerdaniden*, (Bzrk Grdanydn) 66
134	*Dureigh*, (Drygh) 63		
135	*Yek-Guftar*, (Yk Gftar) 63	139	*Beeron*, (Byrun) 66
136	*Ora Dur Awurd Az Doo ꝛud*,	140	*Chĕ Arzoo Daree ?* (Chh Arzu Dary ?) 67

N. B. Of the other engraved Specimens, the explanations immediately follow the Plates, excepting that of the Frontispiece, which is explained in the last Chapter. Throughout the following pages, wherever I have followed the Persian orthography, the letter *Sa*, is expressed by S; *Jim*, by J; *Chim*, by Ch; *Hha*, by Hh, or *h* single; *Kha*, by Kh; *Zal*, by Z; *Za*, by Z; *Sſad*, by S; *Zzad*, by Z; *Ain*, by *a, or æ*; *Ghain*, by Gh; *Vaw*, by U; and *Ya*, by Y.

PERSIAN

نتج ⁶	اسم ¹²	اس ¹⁸	عش ²⁴	دور ³⁰	نج ³⁶
تجذل ⁵	تمثل ¹¹	افس ¹⁷	مرغ ²³	در ²⁹	دس ³⁵
ت ⁴	زن ¹⁰	کسنی ¹⁶	اش ²²	کی ²⁸	دوسه ³⁴
ب ³	است ⁹	گان ¹⁵	کبر ²¹	زنی ²⁷	نیر ³³
اسم ²	در ⁸	س ¹⁴	بکر ²⁰	تنی ²⁶	سکر ³²
کن ¹	کل ⁷	اژن ¹³	عط ¹⁹	م ²⁵	دژ ³¹

سر	ترن	ـع	ال	لہ	ےر
اکدی	حسرون	شہ	حر	اجن	رر
کنک	اوت	طن	رے	کلس	ادر
ط	حقی	حرا	زنست	سر	اںی
حر	کس	وم	لحر	عکر	سو
سلں	ترں	ترں	الحن	ترں	حزں

Plate III.

Plate IV.

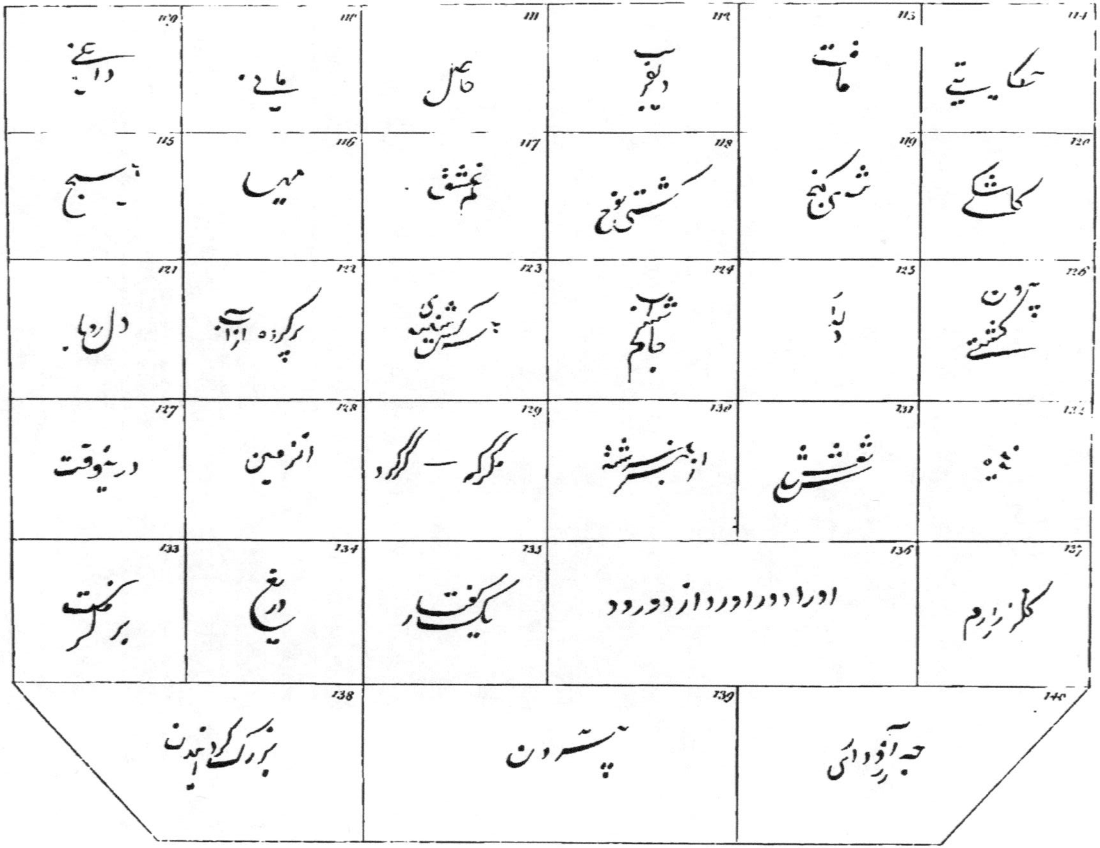

PERSIAN MISCELLANIES.

AN ESSAY

TO

FACILITATE THE READING OF

PERSIAN MANUSCRIPTS.

CHAPTER I.

GENERAL OBSERVATIONS.

WHEN the religion of Mohammed was impofed on the conquered Perfians, the language of Arabia and the Korân became their general and favourite ftudy. Then commenced a flight intertexture of Arabic words (which time has by degrees more firmly incorporated) with thofe of the pure *Deri*,

B or

or original Court dialect of Perſia; and, through the medium of the regular *Niſkhi* hand-writing, we may trace the form of the upright *Cufick*, (the proper character of the ancient Arabs) in the graceful flouriſhes of the Perſian *Talik*, and even in the uncouth combinations of the *Shekesteh* hand. But ſo few and immaterial are the variations which have affected either the Perſian letters or language, for many centuries, that a perfect knowledge of the dialect and character uſed by modern writers, will be found a ſufficient qualification for thoſe who would peruſe the ancient and moſt admired authors. To that particular form of writing I ſhall therefore confine my obſervations in the following pages; nor ſhall I dwell on thoſe myſterious characters which compoſe the celebrated *Perſepolitan* inſcriptions, (and which are only to be found amid the ruins of Perſia's ancient capital) ſince all attempts to decipher their meaning have hitherto proved vain, and the moſt learned orientaliſts have afforded little more on the ſubject than conjecture. Yet it is probable that thoſe ſculptured marbles are the too faithful depoſitories of ſome important ſecrets: their inſcriptions may contain records of illuſtrious actions, the memory of which has long been loſt; political regiſters of the mightieſt empire of the world; or religious myſteries, inſcribed in characters known, perhaps, only to a particular order, or certain number of the ſacred function*.

ON

---

* See " Millii (Davidis) Diſſert. (de Fabul. Orient.) p. 77, quarto, Leyden, 1743—and the Works of Hyde, Kæmpfer, &c.—alſo the Travels of Herbert, Chardin.

CHAP. I.]   PERSIAN MISCELLANIES.   3

On the subject of the *Pehlavi*, and language of the *Zend*, now almoſt extinct in Perſia, and of the characters in which the ſuppoſed works of *Zeràtuſht*, or Zoroaſter, have been written, I refer the reader to the learned obſervations of Hyde and Jones *.

Of the various kinds of hand-writing at preſent in uſe among the Perſians, the principal are

The *Niſkhi*— نسخي (which ſignifies *a tranſcript*);

The *Tâlik*— تعليق (or *hanging*); and

The *Shekeſteh*— شكسته (or *broken* character):

With

Le Bruyn, and Niebuhr—The " Eſſai ſur l'Hiſtoire du Sabeïſme," by the Baron de Bock, quarto, 1787, Halle; and duodecimo, 1788, Metz.—who aſcribes to the venerable ruins of Perſepolis a degree of antiquity of more than three thouſand years before the Chriſtian Æra—and he is of opinion that " *leurs inſcriptions dans une langue qu'en regarde comme perdue, peuvent mener aux découvertes les plus nouvelles et les plus intereſſantes.*"—Conſult alſo the " Quatuor Opuſcula Antiquitates Orientales illuſtrantia," of the learned Swediſh Profeſſor Tychſen, Roſtoch, 1794, quarto.—And finally, the " Memoires ſur diverſes Antiquités de la Perſe", by A. J. Silveſtre de Sacy; a rare and valuable work.

M. Le Bruyn has given a great variety of drawings; and Niebuhr is juſtly celebrated for his accuracy: but the copiouſneſs and univerſal information of Chardin leave him ſtill the firſt in rank among oriental travellers. The fineſt general view, however, that I have ſeen, of the remains of Perſepolis, is that given by the " Heer Herbert de Jager, 1693, in the Dutch Collection of Voyages, by Valentyn, 5 vol. folio, 1724, 1726: the plate is entitled, " Ruinen van t' paleis van Darius.

* An alphabet, and ſpecimens of the ancient Perſian, are given in the ſecond edition of " Hydes Religio Vetorum Perſarum," and many curious remarks on the *Pehlavi*,

the

4   PERSIAN MISCELLANIES.   [CHAP. I.

With the firſt of theſe the reader is ſuppoſed to be already acquainted, from the alphabet given in the Arabic and Perſian Grammars, and from the peruſal of other printed books; and I think it unneceſſary to make particular mention of thoſe hands called, *Kirma, Shulſi, Dewani, Yakoot, Togra*, and ſuch others *; becauſe they rarely occur in Perſian manuſcripts; and, being only variations of the *Niſkhi*, may be eaſily learned at any time by thoſe acquainted with that character, which, by the natives of India, who ſeldom uſe it, is called *Nuſkh*, and written without the final Y; but by Erpenius, Jones, Richardſon, and the Arabian, Perſian, and Turkiſh Grammarians, it is pronounced *Niſkhi*, and ſpelt accordingly.

THE ſecond-mentioned hand, or *Talik*, ſhall be the ſubject of the following pages: for the uſe of the third, or *Shekeſteh*, is almoſt totally confined to familiar correſpondence (and eſpecially among the Indians) or works written in extreme hurry, intended merely as rough copies, from which at leiſure tranſcripts might be made in the more elegant *Talik*.

So confuſed, inaccurate, and uncouth is the *Shekeſteh* hand, and ſo much has it degenerated from the parent *Niſkhi*, that many even among the natives of Hindooſtàn (as I have been aſſured in letters from an ingenious friend long reſident there)

the *Zend*, and *Perſepolitan* inſcriptions in Sir William Jones's Anniverſary Diſcourſe on the Perſians, 1789.

* See the various Arabic Grammars, and Kæmpfer's moſt ingenious work, the "Amænitates Exoticæ," p. 145. Lemgoviæ. 4to. 1712.

are

CHAP. I.]   PERSIAN MISCELLANIES.   5

are puzzled for hours in striving to decipher particular words, and, after all, are probably indebted to the context for their success in ascertaining the sense. Notwithstanding this, a previous knowledge of the *Talik* hand, which holds a middle place between the regular *Niskhi* and broken *Shekesteh*, will render any person master of the latter in a little time; and, that a perfect knowledge of it is absolutely necessary to those whom business obliges to reside in the East, will appear from the testimonies of those writers whom I have quoted in the note *.

IF I might here suggest the subject for a future work, and presume to offer the Essay now before the reader as a model, I would venture to affirm that few publications would be more acceptable to the Persian scholar, obliged by business or publick situation to visit India, than a discussion and analysis of the chief difficulties in the common *Shekesteh* hand, in which all the letters of that country are written, all accounts kept, and commerce carried on; the engraved specimens of such a work should be (after a few plates of single words) letters from princes, generals, and merchants, on trade, negociations, money transactions, orders, reports, &c. all composed in the usual style and language of the country, and given also in the *Niskhi* or *Talik* hand. Such specimens, well translated and illustrated

* Jones's Persian Grammar, Pref. 16, and p. 147; Richardson's Arabic Grammar, p. 2; and Mr. Hadley (the teacher of Persian writing and orthography) in his grammatical remarks prefixed to the " Persian Vocabulary," p. 12.

with

with notes, would not only promote the chief object of the work, by rendering the character familiar, but would give the learner, at the same time, a knowledge of local manners and customs, furnish him with many phrases used in commercial, military, and civil transactions; and would speedily qualify him for entering into business with the natives of Hindooſtàn.

To the want of regularity, the omiſſion of points, and the confuſion that characterize this inelegant species of writing, we may juſtly aſcribe many of the errors found in Perſian manuſcripts, beautifully written in the *Talik* hand; eſpecially in thoſe which have been imported from India. For there, to ſave the expenſe of purchaſing, the poorer *Munſhies*, (teachers and writers) borrow the fine manuſcripts of *Iraun*, or Perſia, and having haſtily tranſcribed them in their inaccurate *Shekeſteh*, lend one to another theſe defective copies, which they again tranſcribe, with all their errors, into fair *Talik*, decorate them probably with miniature paintings and ſplendid decorations, and vend them for their ſubſiſtence *. But more learned perſonages than the poor Indian Munſhies have been led into groſs errors, by adopting the inaccuracies of Arabian and Perſian ſcribes †.

I MUST

---

* Chardin attributes the defects of Perſian MSS. to the ignorance and inattention of the copyiſts, who ſeldom take the trouble of reading over what they have written—" ces fautes arrivent par l'ignorance des copiſtes, &c. &c. Vol. III. p. 150.

† Dr. Hyde, in his admirable notes on the Rabbinical work, which he tranſlated under the title of " *Itinera Mundi*," has detected many miſtakes of this nature, p. 32.

" Et

CHAP. I.]   PERSIAN MISCELLANIES.   7

I MUST here remark, that in India the *Talik* hand is generally called *Nustaleek*, and written accordingly with the letters *Nun* and *Sin* prefixed. Although ufed occafionally by the Arabian, and commonly by the Turkifh penmen, yet it feems to be more particularly a favourite of the Perfians *. In it are written the works of all their poets and authors, of almoft every defcription: in fhort, it may be faid, that in the *Talik* hand are enveloped all the beauties of Perfick literature; and fuch lovers of fcience are the ftudious Perfians (as a celebrated French traveller informs us) that *writing*, its chief vehicle, is efteemed among them as one of their moft noble and liberal arts †.

―――――

" Et quidem quomodo literarum inter fe invicem fimilitudinem nominum et vocum confufionem peperit conftat tam ex plurimis aliis, quam vice verfa ex mutatione, fyllabæ," &c. He points out and correcfs an error in the celebrated Lexicon, called *Kamús*, occafioned by miftaking a final *N* for the the letter *R*, irregularly joined to a final *H*. He alfo correcfs a fimilar error in the Perfian Tables, publifhed by the learned Greaves, and others of various orientalifts—Itinera Mundi, 4to. Oxon. 1691. Pockocke, Bochart, &c. &c. See alfo, " Rhenferdii opera Philolog. 4to, Utrecht, 1722.

* " Secundum (fcripturæ genus) *Taälik*, quo Perfæ utuntur," &c. Erpenii Gr. Arab. 4. " Magis tamen Pendulo et involuto charactere quam Arabes utuntur qui propterea *Khett' Talik* vocatur, unde fcripturæ lectu paulò·difficilior exurgit. Gravii Gram. Perf. p. 4. This paffage, almoft verbatim, Father Angelo gives as his own, in the Intr. Gaz. Perf.

† " Or comme ils font favans et qu'ils aiment fort la fcience il arrive qui l'art de l'Ecriture, eft un des leurs plus nobles'arts liberaux et celui dont ils font le plus de cas," Chardin, Vol. III. p. 150.

PERSIAN MISCELLANIES.   [Chap. I.

We find accordingly, that Calligraphy, or fine penmanſhip, has been long cultivated in Perſia, with ſo much ſuccefs, that this hand, which peculiarly affects graceful flouriſhes and combinations of letters, has been improved to a degree of conſummate elegance; and the beauty of this character gives occaſion to a moſt learned orientaliſt, of celebrating the variety and luxuriance of the Eaſtern pen, and the wonderful fertility of Aſiatic imagination*.

When employed in tranſcribing the works of their favourite poets, romances, or narratives of heroick atchievements, the Perſian ſcribes exhibit ſuch minute neatneſs of execution, ſuch taſte in the combination of letters, a variety of fancy ſo ſplendid in the diſpoſition of the ornamental parts, that a volume containing the productions of any celebrated author, written by a capital artiſt in his beſt manner, and furniſhed with miniatures and illuminations of adequate brilliancy, brings, even in the Eaſt, a price which will appear extravagant to an European, acquainted only with the current value of printed books.

In a very ingenious work, lately tranſlated from the Perſian, we learn that a few manuſcripts, written in a beautiful hand, conſtituted no inconſiderable part of a moſt magnificent offer-

---

* " ———— " Mirari elegantem varietatem, &c."—" Sed hæ ſunt Orientis opes; hæc luxuria ſtis calami et ſcitilis imaginationis in gentibus Aſiaticis indicia," &c. &c. p. 239. Relandi Differt. Miſcell. Vol. III. de Gemmis Arab. Theſe volumes contain a variety of m ſt lear el and irg i us diſſertations on Eaſtern literature and antiquities.

ing

CHAP. I.]   PERSIAN MISCELLANIES.   9

ing from a conquered prince to the triumphant monarch *Nadir Shah* *; and a single volume, brought from India by an English gentleman, some years ago, was purchased at the exorbitant rate of one thousand rupees †. It is not, however, always found that the most highly ornamented manuscripts are written with the greatest accuracy, or that they present the most authentic readings: yet we can hardly suppose that much pains would be taken to render beautiful, that which is known to be eminently defective. The most ancient manuscripts, I believe, or those written nearest the time of the original authors, will be found in general the most correct; because, from the inattention of the transcribers already mentioned, each succeeding copyist adds errors of his own to those of his predecessors. So that the latest transcript will be an aggregate of all their faults, unless written with peculiar care, and collated with many other copies of the same work.

---

* This superb present consisted, among other valuable articles, of the conquered Prince's diadem, three hundred camels, two hundred horses, twenty Persian manuscripts, most beautifully written, &c. &c. The books were given in charge to the secretary of state. See Mr. Gladwin's Memoirs of Khojeh Abdul Kerrum, a Cashmerian of distinction. P. 46. duodecimo, 1793.

† About one hundred and twenty-five pounds. This valuable manuscript was brought to England by General Carnac; who lent it, with many others, to Mr. Richardson, the learned author of the Arabic and Persian Dictionary. It was a miscellaneous collection of extracts from the most celebrated writers, decorated in the Eastern manner, with paintings of the warriors and princesses, the heroes and heroines of the poems. Richardson's Dissertations, p. 350, octavo, second edition, Oxford, 1778.

C   On

On the subject of those splendid decorations and brilliant paintings, which so much enhance the value of Persian manuscripts, I shall offer in another place some observations: in the present essay my design is merely to assist the learner, by a few remarks on the combinations of letters used in the *Tâlik* hand, and explanations of its most obvious difficulties and irregularities. And, before I present the reader with any specimens of Persian writing, I shall make some observations, separately, on the letters of the alphabet, in the usual order; marking their principal deviations from the regular *Niskhi* hand, and the different combinations and contractions incidental to them.

CHAPTER II.

PARTICULAR OBSERVATIONS ON THE LETTERS OF THE ALPHABET.

ALIF.

WITH this letter, from its simple upright figure, the penman can, perhaps, take fewer liberties than with any other of the alphabet: we find, however, that some irregularities attend it in respect to its situation and place among the other letters of a word; thus in books hastily transcribed it is sometimes found, though initial, joined to, and as it were pendent from the next letter; as in the word *Aunchunàn*, thus so, &c. No. 1. of the first plate[*]: and in the middle, or other parts, as in *Seranjaum*, the end, conclusion, &c. No. 2: or over the other letters, as in *Auncheh*, that which, whoever, &c. No. 3. It is often placed under the other component letters of a syllable, which it begins, as in the word *Eſt* or *Aſt*, he is, it is, &c. No. 4: and in *Iſtikbaùl*, futurity, meeting, &c. No. 5: also when not initial, as in *Daſhtun*, to have, No. 6: and it is

[*] The original orthography of all the words given in the four first plates, will be found in the index prefixed to the first chapter of this work.

frequently placed perpendicularly over the *R* of the syllable that marks the oblique case, as in the word *Gulra*, from *Gul*, a flower, a rose, No. 7; or any other word in which that syllable occurs, as in *Bokhara*, the name of a city, No. 8. I have seen two Alifs thus placed under the two last letters of *Aumedest*, he has come, &c. No. 9: Alif is sometimes joined to a succeeding letter, with a curved tail*, as in *Firaukh* large, abundant, &c. No. 10: but here it must be remarked, that the curve of the final *Kha*, was brought by a prolongation of the flourish (which is esteemed a beauty) to unite thus with the properly unconnected *Alif*.

WE find Alif sometimes irregularly connected with other letters, as with *D* in the word *Shimshad*, the box-tree, No. 11: but this mode of connexion approaches the irregularity of the *Shekesteh* hand; and, for remarks on the improper position and combination of letters, I refer the reader to the fourth chapter, and the explanations of the engraved specimens.

As I before observed, the essential simplicity of this letter's form, secures it from any considerable alterations: I have

---

* I have already mentioned (in the Introduction) the necessity under which all writers have found themselves, of using similar words and phrases, in explanations of this kind: thus Rhenferdius in Rudim. Ling. Or. 832. " Hebræi punctum illud ventri literæ inscribunt:" also " de Charact. Palmyr." 670, &c. Gimel, non tantum capite est diminutum, sed et ipso corpore, remanente solo collo cum pede anteriore, &c. " Daleth, deorsum incurvata et cauda nonnihil aucta, &c." Angelo, in his Gazophylaium Persicum, clavis, p. 3. " Vaw caput crassum habet, et caudam exilem." See also De Dieu's and Greaves's Persian Grammar, and all the other oriental philologists.

only

Chap. II.]   PERSIAN MISCELLANIES.   13

only remarked, that in some manuscripts, the unconnected Alif is often turned a little towards the lower part, as in the word *Dashtun*, to have, No. 6: and that in fine writings, like many other letters, it is frequently described as a mere hair-stroke, as in Nos. 27, 47, 70, 71, 73, 76, 83, 96, 97, and many other instances.

Of the Letters Ba *and* Pa.

Of these letters, the former is generally used by the Persian writers instead of the latter: thus they write *badishah* for *padishah*, a king, No. 13: but no word spelt properly with *ba* is ever written with *pa*. This confusion being occasioned by the substituting one diacritical point for three, I refer the reader to the next chapter of this work, in which they are particularly treated of.

The stroke or body of these characters, when initial, is often so faintly marked, or so immediately blended with the following letter, as to be scarcely discernible, and known only by the diacritical point or points below; as in the words *Bokhara*, a city, No. 8: *besiaur*, many, much, &c. No. 14: *pechegaùn*, infants, No. 15: and *bechcshmbaï*, to the eyes, in the eyes, &c. No. 16: the curve or bow of these letters, when final, is often much contracted at the extremities: thus, in

aftaub,

aftaub, the fun, No. 17: and in *afp**, or *afib*, a horfe, No. 18.

Of the Letter Tᴀ.

This letter, like thofe preceding, is frequently, when initial, fo faintly expreffed, as to be afcertained only by its points: thus in *teftym*, faluting, granting, &c. No. 19: And it is often defcribed by a plain turn of the pen, as in *geety*, the world, No. 20, where it is rounded into the final *ya*, but marked by its diacritical points, alfo in *grifty*, fecond pers. pret. fing. of

---

* Among the ancient Perfians this word appears to have been a very favourite termination of kings and heroes names; *Lohrafp*, *Arjafp*, *Guftafp*, &c. which laft may be eafily recognifed in the Greek *Hyftafpes*; and it is probable that in thefe compounds the original fenfe of the word *Afp* was retained, and that it alluded to or expreffed the national fondnefs for horfes, and fkill in the management of them; which occafioned the Hebrew name פרסאי, *Parfai*, to be applied to the Perfians, who, before the time of Cyrus, the firft encourager of horfemanfhip among them, were ftyled in general *Elamites*. A very flight and hafty perufal of *Ferdufi's* incomparable poem, the *Shahnameh*, or Book of King's, has furnifhed me with the following names of ancient Perfian heroes, all ending in the word *afp*, viz. *Arjafp*, *Jamafp*, *Duhurafp*, *Gurfhafp* or *Gurfafp*, *Guftafp* or *Kiftafp*, *Sheidafp*, *Lohrafp*, and *Tehemafp*; to thefe may be added *Piurafp*, mentioned by D'Herbelôt and *Ibnafp*, by Profeffor *Schikard*, in his *Tarich Regum Perfia*, proem. p. 41. As it would exceed the limits of this note, and belongs more properly to the antiquary or etymologift to dwell on the original compofition of thefe titles, I fhall only here remark that I have not found the word *afp* to conclude the name of any female; and I defer any further obfervations to another time.

grifton,

CHAP II.]   PERSIAN MISCELLANIES.   15

grifton, to take, No. 21, where its points are carelefsly placed at the fide. When neceffary to fill up a line (which is frequently the cafe in tranfcribing poetry, the lines being always of equal length) the letter *ta,* like others, may be extended or prolong'd at pleafure, as in the word *auftadeh,* fallen, &c. No. 22. On the fubject of the points which alone diftinguifh this letter from *Ba, Pa, Sa, Nun,* and *Ya* in many inftances, the reader muft confult the third chapter.

Of the Letter SA.

ITS three diacritical points alone diftinguifh this letter from that laft treated of; when final it is often much curved, in the fame manner as *Ba,* and *Pa* which I before defcribed, of this an example occurs in the word *Hedees*—a ftory, event, narration, &c. No. 23.

Of the Letters JIM and CHIM.

THESE characters, like *Ba* and *Pa,* are fo far confounded by the Perfian writers, that the former with one point is generally fubftituted for the latter, which fhould be defcribed with three: thus they often write the letter *Chim* in *Chefhm*

(the

(the eye) with one point only, No. 24: alfo in *bechefhm hay*, before quoted, No. 16. But they never fpell with *chim*, and its three points, a word which properly begins with *Jim*.

These letters are often rounded inftead of being pointed or expreffed by an acute angle, as in *Suranjaum*, end, conclufion, &c. No. 2; and in *cheh* what, how, &c. No. 25; alfo in *chun*, when, No. 102. A little crofs ftroke is fometimes ufed to divide and diftinguifh thefe letters from *Sin* and *Shin*, when the latter are expreffed by a long dafh of the pen as they moft commonly are in the *Talik* hand; thus in the compound word *bechefhm hay*, to the eyes, &c. No. 16. When *chim* is defcribed with three points, they are often confufed and blended together, as in *pechegaun*, infants, No. 15.

Of the Letters Hha *and* Kha.

The fame combinations nearly affect thefe letters as the two preceding: like thofe, they are often fomewhat rounded both when initial and in the middle or other parts of a word, as in *Hedees*, a ftory, &c. No. 23: *Sekhun*, a word, difcourfe, &c. No. 28. And in *Zeleekha*, No. 27, the name of a woman, the celebrated miftrefs of Jofeph, the Hebrew Patriarch, whofe loves are the fubject of a moft admirable Perfian Romance, written in the fineft verfe by *Molla Abd errahman*
ben

CHAP. II.] PERSIAN MISCELLANIES. 17

ben Ahmed Jàmi, who flourished in the ninth century of the Mahometan Æra*. From this poet's works, of which I am fortunate in possessing two beautiful manuscripts, the reader will find some extracts in the course of the following pages. Among many other excellent productions, he is chiefly admired as the author of the Romance, above mentioned: the *Beharistan* or Residence of Spring—and his *Divaun* or Collection of Odes and Sonnets; from the *Beharistan*, some fables and sentences have been published with a Latin translation†, but of the poems collected in his Divaun, one only, I believe, has yet appeared in any European dress‡. It is not, perhaps, generally known, that there existed, of this surname, two poets

---

* *Jàmi* derived this Sirname from his native Village *Jàm*, and died about the year 1486 of our Æra, according to Mr. D'Herbelôt, in his Bibliotique Orientale: article *Giami*—I quote the Edition of this admirable work, published in four Quarto Volumes at the Hague 1777, 1782— with a fine engraving of the Author's head prefixed to the first, and the additions of the late Professor Scheltens of Leyden at the end of the fourth Volume. "The Divaun of Jàmi", says Mr. D'Herbelôt, "is in a style *du genre sublime, et contient toute la théologie mystique des Musulmans*"—after this, the repartee ascribed to him in the same article, will surprise those who understand the equivocal meaning of the original Persian.

† In the " Anthologia Persica"—4to. Vienna, 1778. In which very ingenious work the reader will find an account of the Poet Jàmi, and a list of all his writings, wherein are enumerated above forty compositions of this very fertile author.

‡ See the " Magazin für Alte besonders Morgen landische und Biblische Litteratur.' twiete lieferung. 8vo. Cassel, p. 138, 1789. A periodical work of merit, but soon discontinued.

D   in

in the same century: but of the superior excellence of the author of "*Joseph and Zeleekha*" and "the *Beharistan*", we require not a more convincing proof than the total omission of the other *Jàmi* by the learned Herbelôt, and the very slight mention of his existence, and his name by the ingenious *Wahl*, to whom we are indebted for the German version of the poem before mentioned.

AND before I present it to the reader under another form, I must observe, that the Divan of Jàmi, which contains, according to Mr. D'Herbelôt, all the mystick theology of the Mahometans, is replete with passages of the most tender and amorous description—and, with an inconsistence by no means unfrequent among the Persian writers, religious Poems of a sublime and mysterious nature, are comprised in the same work with Erotick and Bacchanalian Odes and Sonnets; and the same person appears, as we read his different compositions, the enthusiastic and bigotted devotee, the gay, voluptuous, or impassioned lover, equally content to resign his existence for the sake of his God, his prophet, or his mistress*.

---

* "The excesses of enthusiasm (to use the words of a learned and elegant writer) have "been observed in every age to lead to sensual gratifications, the same constitution that "is susceptible of the former, being remarkably prone to the latter."

Dr. Robertson's History of Charles V. Vol. 2, 381. The extraordinary actions and tenets of many religious Sectaries a few centuries ago, confirm the observation of this excellent historian.

CHAP. II.]   PERSIAN MISCELLANIES.   19

But the poet, whom I particularly speak of, whether he pours forth the ejaculations of piety and devotion, or breathes the sentiments of paffion, or the fondeft love, is found to have uniformly maintained the greateft correctnefs and chaftity of language; neither has he been influenced by the example of two moft celebrated writers to pollute his pages with fuch grofs indelicacies as have ftained the claffic volume of *Anvàri*, nor to admit into his Divàun fuch compofitions as *Sadi* very juftly ftyled " *his Impurities*," and which the aftonifhed and difgufted reader can fcarcely believe to have fallen from that poet's moral pen—yet *Anvàri* is fpoken of as the firft who corrected the exceffive licentioufnefs of Perfian poetry, and *Sadi* is univerfally celebrated for his inftructive leffons of Morality and Virtue*.

In the Lyric compofitions of Perfia, we do not always find a regular feries of thoughts, or fucceffion of ideas: they frequently confift of feveral unconnected images and fentiments independent of each other; nor has the Sonnet already fpoken of, from the Divaun of Jamì, been chofen by the tranflator as an exception to this remark. From the German verfion of it, which is literal, a very ingenious friend in Holland compofed,

---

* See D'Herbelôt, Bibl. Orient. art. *Anvàri*—and fome account of the Poet Sadi in the courfe of this work.

D 2   almoft

almoſt extempore, a poetical Latin paraphraſe, which on ſome future occaſion I ſhall preſent the reader. The following Gazzel or Elegiac Sonnet of Jami, I have choſen as a ſpecimen of that plaintive Poet's ſtyle.

SONNET.

From the Perſian of Jami.

* " Dejected and melancholy I fly to unfrequented places:
" The city without thee becomes irkſome—I ſeek the ſolitude of the deſart.

> * " Sooee Schrauny bee yſh u temaſha miveem,
> " Ree too ber men Shuber teuk anmed beſhra mireom.
> " Ta too reſty az ber'em ba kes uedavem ulſity,
> " Ghur cheh laſhud ſad kes'em bemrah, tenha mireom.
> " Heich jaee az wehiſhet tenhaye'm nebuzed mulal;
> " Moowes'i jaune'm kheyal't eſt, ber ja mi room.
> " Pa be zungeer bala her ſoo tulb i kav t:o am,
> " Arflik danwauneh am, zungeer ber pa mireom.
> " Fi al miſl gher zeer poï men bud gul ya berer;
> " Ghir neh ſaee t.ſt rah, ber Khar u Khara mireom.
> " Geſtem, aï janu roo, leh bee jaunaun nekhankem zendegy:
> " Geſt, Jami, ſebr kun, k'invosz u ſerda mireom."

The original Perſian of this Sonnet I ſhall give in a future publication, with ſeveral other lyric compoſitions of Jami, Sadi, Hafiz, Caſſim, Anvari, Khoſroo, Senaï, &c. &c. hitherto unpubliſhed.

" Since

CHAP. II.]   PERSIAN MISCELLANIES.   21

" Since you have forsaken this constant bosom, I have been a stranger to all
  " fond affections;
" Though surrounded by an hundred friends, I feel myself alone.

" Yet in the drearinefs of the defart I feel not the affliction of folitude;
" Wherefoever I wander thy beloved image is the companion of my foul.

" Loaden with thy chains I feek thee on every fide,
" Bound with the fetters of love, a diftracted wretch!

" It is alike to me, whether rofe-leaves were fcattered, or filken carpets fpread
  " beneath my feet:
" If the road lead not to thee, I fhould feem to walk amid fharp thorns and rug-
  " ged rocks.

" I faid unto my vital fpirit, " Leave me!—I will exift no longer without
  " her I love;"
" It replied, "O Jami! a while be patient; thy life is on the eve of departure."

As I fhall have occafion hereafter, to quote the poet *Jami*, I fhall dwell no longer in this place on his writings, but return to the original fubject of my Effay: the graphical difficulties of Perfian MSS.: and of the letter *Kha*, I fhall here remark, though it more properly belongs to the next chapter, that in fome writings, from the irregular pofition of the point of *Kha*, (being either too high above the line, or placed over fome other part of the word) a learner may be perplexed to afcertain the letter to which it belongs, as in the example laft quoted, *Zeleekha*, No. 27: where it appears at firft, as if placed over

the

the body of *Ya*, which it would then constitute an *N*. Also in *Sekhun*, a word, discourse, &c. No. 28.

Of the Letter DAL.

IN many manuscripts, negligently written, this letter is very slightly distinguished from *Ra*, but it is generally made at the upper part a little thicker and more curved, as in that word of very frequent occurrence, *der*, in, into, a gate, &c. No. 29. It is sometimes also written so carelessly as not to be easily distinguished from the letter *Vaw*, but even in that case it will be found, on close inspection, that the head of the latter is much rounder and larger than the upper part of *Dal*, as in the word *doft* or *düft* a friend, a mistress, &c. No. 30. How this letter should differ from *Ra*, and *Vaw*, will best appear from the following example in which the three letters are found: viz. *Rud*, he goes, the third pers. present. sing. of the verb *Rooiden*, or *Raviden*, to go; or a noun substantive signifying a river, the string of a musical instrument, &c. No. 31.

FROM this example it will appear that to describe the *Dal*, it is necessary to lean on the pen at the top of the letter, and finish with a slighter stroke: whilst in writing the *Ra*, one should begin slightly and lean more heavily towards the tail—differing from both, the letter *Vaw*, must have a rounder and

CHAP. II.] PERSIAN MISCELLANIES. 23

and larger head, which will be moſt eaſily expreſſed by a kind of circular motion of the pen.

BUT at the end of ſyllables connected, *Dal* does not always obſerve the rule of having the head or upper part more ſtrongly mark'd than the lower, as in *Skander*, No. 32—the name of Alexander the Great, whoſe victory over Dara, or Darius, his conqueſt of Perſia, his other heroic actions, and his amours, are celebrated in moſt excellent poetry by *Nizàmi**.

ALSO in *Neſhayed*, it is not fit, meet, &c. No. 33.

Dal is ſometimes improperly joined to another letter by a long ſtroke, as in *Zoormend*, powerful, ſtrong, &c. No. 34.

IT is alſo frequently connected with a final *ha*, which it involves in the extremity of its flouriſh, as in *Mandeh*, remained, redundant, &c. No. 35.

AFTER ſome letters, it appears often more like the termination of the preceding letter than a diſtinct character, as in *Hedys*, news, tradition, &c. No. 23: *Hind*, India, No. 38.

IN the word *Shimſhad*, the box tree, No. 11, the *Dal*, final, is joined to the preceding *Alif*, in a manner as I before

---

* Of five different copies in my poſſeſſion, of this admirable poem, three are compriſed with the other works of *Nizàmi*, highly decorated with paintings and ſplendidly illuminated—but not ſo valuable, in my opinion, as the other two plainer but more accurate copies, which are ſingle volumes, enrich'd with marginal and interlinear notes, explaining many obſcure and difficult paſſages—for ſome remarks on this work, and the poet *Nizàmi*, I refer the reader to the fifth and ſixth chapters of this Eſſay.

remarked

remarked, refembling the *Shekefteh* hand. And in a Manufcript before me, very coarfely written, the final *Dal*, is fometimes moft uncouthly inverted, as in the word *Shud*, was, (upper figure) No. 39 : (for the lower figure fee remarks on the letter *ha*.)

The Letter ZAL,

As Mr. Richardfon, obferves in his Dictionary, begins only one word in the Perfian language* but it occurs in the middle of many, and at the beginning of words originally Arabic, of which great numbers are introduced into the Perfian writings—I have only remarked of this letter, that it is generally more curved, and rather larger than the *Dal*, from which, however, its diacritical point is, in fact, the fole diftinction, as in *Izaur*, the face, &c. No. 40.

Of the Letter RA.

As I before obferved, (fee the letter *Dal*,) this character fometimes refembles the D. but it is generally thinner at the top than that letter, and fomewhat lefs curved ; as in *Der* No 29 ; and *Rud*, No. 31, both before quoted.—It is often defcribed as a mere hairftroke ; thus in *Murd*, a Man, No. 41 ;

* *Zulam*, the Iliack paffion, the cholic.

and

[CHAP. II.] PERSIAN MISCELLANIES.

and frequently without any curve, as in *Gohurhay*, jewels, No. 71; and in the compound *beher*, to, or in all, every, &c. No. 42, where the reader will find three several ways of writing that word.

Of the Letter ZA *and* ZHA.

THE points alone diſtinguiſh theſe letters from the preceding *Ra*, and from each other, as in *Zerdhuſht*, the name of the great prophet and chief of the Perſian Magi, No. 43.*

Za, is known from *Zal* by being leſs curved: and like *Ra*, it is often expreſſed as a mere ſtraight hair-ſtroke, thus in *ghemzeh* a wink, or glance, No. 44.

Of the Letter SIN *and* SHIN.

I bring theſe characters under one head, becauſe they are affected by the ſame combinations, and expreſſed by the ſame flouriſhes—So much have theſe letters deviated from the original regularity of figure as not to be recogniſed without difficulty by the mere reader of plain *Niſkhi*, or printed character. For, in the firſt place,

---

* I have followed the manner of writing this name in a manuſcript before me; it is, however, ſpelt in different ways by the Perſians, and Sir Wm. Jones, writes it *Zerátuſht*.—See alſo Hyde, Herbelôt, &c. &c.

PERSIAN MISCELLANIES.   [Chap. II.

Their indentures are generally quite fmoothed away, and they are defcribed by a fimple dafh of the pen : as in the words *Sèaub*, black, No. 45 : *Gulsher*, a rofe-garden, No. 46; *Solyman*, a proper name, No. 47; *Shud*, was, (the upper fig.) No. 39 : and *Sheh* for *Shah*, a King, the lower figure of the fame number.

Of thefe letters the flourifh or dafh is often fomewhat waving or ferpentine, as in *Sâdi*, the celebrated poet's name, No. 48 ; *Solyman*, above quoted, No. 47 ; and *Shirauz*, No. 49, the name of a famous city in Perfia, the birth place of the poet's *Hafiz*, and *Sâdi*, and remarkable for its fine gardens, wine, and beautiful women*.

From the number of learned men who have iffued from its fchools, the honourable title of the "Perfian Athens," has been beftowed by a celebrated Orientalift† on this claffic city, which, as we are affured by an intelligent traveller of the laft century, was fo fertile in luxuries of every kind, as to give occafion to the Perfian faying, "that if Mohammed had tafted

---

* The lovely nymphs of Shirauz have been celebrated in the fineft ftrains of poetry by *Hafiz* and *Sâdi*, who have both, indeed, done juftice to the produce of its vineyards— Our early travellers have delighted in defcribing its magnificent Gardens, Pietro della Valle, Olearius, Herbert, Dr. Fryer, &c.—the learned Schikard in the introduction to his *Tarich* or Chronicle, celebrates the rofes of *Shirauz;* and the ingenious Kempfer (in Amenit. Exot. 379) ranks the wine of that delightful foil among the fineft in the world.

† The Baron Revicfky, in his " Specimen Poeseös Perficæ" 8vo. Vindob. 1771.

" the

CHAP. II.]   PERSIAN MISCELLANIES.   27

" the pleasures of Shirauz, he would have begged of God to make him immortal there*"; and a celebrated French writer quotes another popular saying which implies, that "When this city was itself (in its original splendour) the great town of Cairo was only as a suburb to it†".

AN English traveller, Sir Thomas Herbert, in his description of this enchanting soil, declares that it realizes the charming idea of Tibullus's Elysium, and quotes the Roman Poet's words.

"Hic Choreæ cantusque vigent passimque vagantes
"Dulce Sonant tenui gutture carmen aves:
"Fert casiam non culta Seges: totosque per agros,
"Florat odoratis terra benigna rosis."

AND he concludes his extravagant encomium on this city with some English verses, in which he compares it to the Garden of Eden, and his own departure from it, to the banishment of Adam from the delights of Paradise.

BUT it is to be feared that the struggles of contending princes for the diadem of Persia, which have convulsed for many years, and still agitate every part of that extensive empire, have effaced all vestiges of the magnificence and luxuries of Shirauz, as of its rival city Ispahàn—the former, as I have been assured by an ingenious foreigner, lately returned from the

* Mr. Mandelslo, among the travels of the Ambassadors.   † Chardin, Vol. II. 203.

E 2   East,

28   PERSIAN MISCELLANIES.   [CHAP. II.

East, presents a most striking picture of decay and perfect desolation: but of the latter, if we may believe a recent French writer*, the ruin is not yet complete: although Shirauz cannot aspire to hope that another Hafiz shall there sing the praises of his native city, celebrate the charms of her black-eyed daughters, and render immortal by his poetry the verdant banks of *Rocknabâd*, and the rosy bowers of *Mosellay*: yet it may be hoped that of *Ispahan*'s former greatness, much is still retrieveable, and that she may yet produce another *Kemaledden* to record her fall†.

THE letters *Sin* and *Shin*, are sometimes expressed by a simple straight line, as in *Lashkuresh*, his army, No. 50—when two *Sins*, *Sin* and *Shin*, or two *Shins* are immediately connected, one is distinguished from the other by the deeper indentures of the former, its being a finer stroke or by a small mark with the pen between, like that between *Chim* and *Shin*, in the word *becheshmhay*, No. 16. See also *Khoosheft*, it is sweet, agreeable, &c. No. 51.

When preceding a final *ta*, and other letters, the indentures are generally somewhat marked, or else the letter is expressed by a plain stroke, finer than that of the following: as in *Dost* or *duset*, a friend, mistress, &c. No. 30: *Zerd-*

* M. de Sauveboeuf," Voyage en Perse, &c. 2 Vols. 12mo. 1790.
† See D'Herbelôt Bibliot. Orient. article Kemaleddin.

husht,

Chap. II.] PERSIAN MISCELLANIES. 29

bufht, a proper Name, No. 43; *imſheb*, to night, No. 52, and *eſt*, it is, No. 4.

The ſtrokes of theſe letters are often ſo blended with thoſe of a preceding or following character, as to aſſume the appearance of a curve or bow; thus in the word *Neſhayed*, it is not fit, &c. No. 33; and in *Gulſhen* a roſe garden, No. 46: they are ſometimes connected with *Lam*, or other letters, in ſuch a manner that they appear as if proceeding from the upper part of the latter: thus in *Gulſhen* before quoted, No. 46: and in the words " *az andiſheh dileſh*," from the thoughts of her heart, No. 103: where the laſt word is above the line*.

From many combinations theſe letters aſſume a very whimſical appearance, which, without previous ſtudy, a beginner cannot well account for: but Time renders ſuch figures eaſy and familiar: as in the word *Sekhun*, No. 53, a diſcourſe, ſpeech, &c. where the initial *Sin* is blended with the following *Kha*, this word is written in a more regular manner, No. 28: (See alſo under the letter *Nun*, in this chapter, where No 53, is refered to.)

From the uſing of one point only, for the three of *pa*, the daſh of the letter *Sin*, and the reverſing of the

---

* The index prefixed to the firſt chapter of this work, will point out the pages where this number, and all the others are explained.

final

final *ya*, with the total omiſſion of that letter's diacritical points, the word *peſy*, more, many, &c. No. 54, exhibits an appearance very different from that which it wears when written in the regular *Niſkhi* hand.

Sin (or Shin) is very often abruptly blended with *Ra*, as in the firſt ſyllable of the word *Seranjaum*, the end, &c. No. 2; and in *Meſhryk*, the laſt, No. 66.

As in the Hebrew alphabet, the letter *Shin* ש is only diſtinguiſhed from the *Sin* שׂ by the addition of a point: ſo with the Arabic and Perſian characters of the ſame name, the diacritical points alone conſtitute any difference. For obſervations, therefore, on *Shin*, as affected by its points, I refer the reader to that chapter in which they are particularly treated of.

Of the Letters Ssad *and* Zzad.

The point over the latter of theſe characters alone diſtinguiſhes it from the former; in ſome Manuſcripts theſe letters are haſtily deſcribed as almoſt round, and blended, in a confuſed manner, with that which follows in the lower limb: as in *Neſret*, brightneſs, &c. No. 55: *Sehra*, a deſart, No. 56; and *Hezret*, Majeſty, preſence, &c. No. 57.

Of

Of the Letters TA and ZZA.

THESE letters are not liable to many irregularities: the point over the latter is its only diftinction from the former. They are fometimes abruptly blended with a fucceeding letter: as in the word *tawk*, power, &c. No. 58.

Of the Letters AIN and GHAIN.

In fome MSS. thefe letters when initial are defcribed as nearly round: the extremities being fo much contracted as to form almoft a circle: thus in *Ghemzeh*, a glance, &c. No. 44: *Izaur*, a face, No. 40.

WHEN medial connected, the *Ghain*, if the head be not properly flat and broad, may often be miftaken for the letter *fa*, as in *Nughmet*, harmony, mufic, No. 61.

Of the Letters FA and KAF.

THESE characters are to be known, one from the other, by a fingle point over the former: two being the characteriftic of the latter. But in the writings of the Moors of Barbary, or Weftern Arabs, the letter *Kaf* is defcribed with

one

one point only, and that it may be diſtinguiſhed from *Fa*, the point of the latter is placed under the letter.*

When medial connected, theſe letters are often deſcribed as a circle not filled up, or a figure of *Nought* with us, as in *Iſtickbaul*, No. 5 : *Goſt*, he ſaid, No. 62 : *Hekyket*, truth, reality, No. 63 ; *Aſhuſteh*, enamoured, confounded, &c. No. 64, and other examples.

As I mentioned under *Ghain*, that letter, if too much rounded, may be ſometimes miſtaken for the *fa* medial : as in *Nughmet*, muſic, &c. No. 61. Theſe letters, like many others, may be lengthened at pleaſure, as in *Fermuden*, to command, &c. No. 65.

Final, they are ſometimes deſcribed as a bow or curve, thus in the word *meſhryk*, the Eaſt, No. 66 ; and this curve is often expreſſed with an upright extremity ſo as to appear like an *Alif*, thus in *Tawk*, power, ſtrength, &c. No. 58.

For irregularities of the points, ſee next chapter.

Of the Letters Caf and Gaf.

There are but few manuſcripts in which the Perſian *Gaf* with three points, is diſtinguiſhed from the Arabic *Caf*, which has not any; thus they write *Gulra*, the oblique

---

* " Occidentales Arabes ſeu Mauri τῷ *Kaf* unum tantum punctum imponunt ; unde τῷ " *fe*, ut ab eo diſcernatur, punctum ſubſternunt."——Waſmuth. Arab. Gram. p. 3.

CHAP. II.]   PERSIAN MISCELLANIES.   33

cafe of *Gul** a Rofe, No. 7: *Pechegàn*, Infants, No. 15, and many other inftances—The firft oblique ftroke of this letter is not always joined to its perpendicular one, as in *Leiken*, but, No. 67; and this upper or oblique ftroke is generally the longer of the two, as in the example juft quoted; the word *Yeky*, One, No 68; and *Goft*, he faid, No. 62.

It is fometimes written after the plain *Nifkhi* manner: and is frequently combined with other letters in a form apparently confufed, as in *gumar*, from *gumariden* to gnafh the teeth, to compel, &c. No. 69; and in fome combinations, particularly with *Mim*, it is often fo defcribed as to give the appearance of a *Kha* or *hha* to the fucceeding letter, as in the No. laft quoted, and in the word *Kumanet*, thy bow, &c. No. 70.

The upper or oblique ftroke is often waved a little, as in *Goft*, he faid, No. 62: *Yeky*, One, No. 68, and others. In fome MSS. I have found this upper ftroke defcribed by a little figure fomewhat refembling our capital letter S; as in *Gohurhay*, Jewels, No. 71.

* The word *Gul* fignifies a *flower*, in general, but the Perfians ufe no other, when fpeaking of their favourite, the Rofe;—the word *Gul*, therefore, in this fenfe, fignifies " *the flower*," by way of excellence.——See Kœmpfer's Amœnit. Exotic. p. 374.

The

34   PERSIAN MISCELLANIES.   [Chap. II.

The hook, or lower limb, is sometimes very suddenly blended with a following letter, as in *Yeky*, One, No. 68; and in the common pronoun *Keh*, Who, That, &c. No. 72: also in "*Kishte Noah*," Noah's Ark, No. 118; and this hook to fill up a line, or at the Writer's pleasure is often extended or dilated, as in *Shemochunànk*, So, Thus, &c, No. 73.

The upper stroke of this letter is by mistake or negligence sometimes omitted, as in *Girift*, he took, No. 74; as it is sometimes crossed through the stroke of another letter, as the reader will find exemplified in the fourth chapter.

Of the Letter Lam.

When initial, or connected with others, this letter is sometimes so faintly marked as to be scarcely perceptible; thus in *Lashkur*, an army, No. 75: *Jemaulesh*, his beauty, No. 76; and in the words, "*Az andisheh dilesh*, from the thoughts of her heart," No. 103.

In writing the Arabic word *Allah*,* God, the Persians generally describe the second *Lam* short, as in the exclamation or oath *Wallah*, Oh God! by God! No. 77.

* The name of God, in pure Persian, is *Khoda*, or *Yzed*;—the former evidently was derived from the Assyrian *Gad*, or *Gada* גדא—whom the author of a Hebrew book styles the God of the Greeks, יון גד—which in the same words the Persians would call *Khoda yunanu*; the other "*Ay Sad* vel *Yzed* antiqua lingua guebrorum Deus"—as it is explained in a marginal note by the celebrated traveller Chardin, in a fine manuscript copy of the *Gulistan*, which lately fell into my hands,—See Selden de Diis Syris,—and Millii Diss. de Gad et Meni, 235—237.

The

Chap. II.] PERSIAN MISCELLANIES.

The very simple form of this letter, in every combination, secures it from any extraordinary liberties of the Penman. For its combination with *Alif,* under the title of *Lamalif,* see the end of this chapter.

Of the Letter Mim.

A simple dot, in many manuscripts, serves to express this letter when initial, as in *Ameedum,* my hope, No. 12; and in *Murd,** a man, No. 41—and a medial *Mim,* like an initial, is often nothing more than a very small point or dot scarcely discernible as in the word *Ghemzeh,* a wink, &c. No. 44; and when final, according to the writer's fancy, its tail may be described either long or short, as *Serenjam,* the End, No. 2: *Ameedum,* my hope, No. 12; *Cheshim,* the eye, No. 24, &c. &c. Of initial and final *Mim,* an example is given in *Ameedum,* before quoted, No. 12.

Mim is often blended in a strange manner with other letters: as with initial and final *ha,* in the word *Hemeh,* all, No. 78; where it is written three different ways: also with *ya,* and *alif,* in *Solyman,* a proper name, No. 47: with *shin,* and *ha,* in *Bechesbmhai,* to the Eyes, No. 16; and many other examples.

* Although the Persians have many ways of expressing *Man,* in a general and particular sense, yet I cannot discover that there is any single word, in their language, which possesses the same distinctive power, as the *vir* and *homo* of the Latins; the ἀνηρ and ἄνθρωπος of the Greeks, and the Hebrew איש and אדם

F 2   *Mim*

Mim is often joined to another letter by a long turned ſtroke, as in *Men*, me or mine, No. 79; alſo in the ſame word, No. 80: *Chun men*, like me, when I, &c.

WHEN it is neceſſary to fill up a line, by dilating or prolonging a letter, the head of final *mim* is often very much flattened and extended, as in *Ghem*, grief, or trouble, No. 60: *Niſeem*, a gale, No. 81.

Of the Letter NUN.

THE body or ſtroke of this letter, when initial, is often ſo faintly marked as to be known only by its point: thus in the word *Niſeem*, a gale, breeze, No. 81: *Niſhayed*, it is not fit, No. 33. Alſo in other parts of a word, as in *Auncheh*, that, which, &c. No. 3: *Surenjàm*, the end, concluſion, No. 2.

THE firſt or right-hand ſtroke of final *Nun*, is generally longer than the other, that is, it riſes higher above the line, as in *Daſhtun*, to have, No. 6: *Pechegàn*, infants, No. 15. *Solyman*, a name, No. 47.

AND final *Nun* is ſometimes very ſtrangely deſcribed by a kind of oblique waving ſtroke, marked by the diacritical point, as in *Sekhun*, a word, diſcourſe, &c. No. 53; and *Damen*, a ſkirt, border, &c. No. 82. The two extremities of final *Nun* are often brought ſo cloſe together as nearly to touch the diacritical point—thus in *Sekhun*, a word, No. 28; and in *Leiken*,

CHAP. II.]   PERSIAN MISCELLANIES.   37

but, No. 67. And final *Nun*, is sometimes expressed by a mere plain dash with the point over, thus ⸿

Of the Letter VAW.

I HAVE already mentioned this letter when treating of the *Dal*, to which I refer the reader. For some further remarks, let him consult the fourth chapter.

Of the Letter HA.

THERE is not, I believe, in the Arabic or Persian alphabet, any letter which assumes, in every situation, a greater variety of forms than the letter *ha*.—It is sometimes expressed by a little upright figure resembling our comma reversed, as in *Mahy*, a fish, No. 83. *Zerdhusht* * Zoroaster, No. 43: and the first *ha* in *Gohurhay*, jewels, No. 71.

---

* Of this great prophet of ancient Persia, (whose name has been spelt several ways) the Life at large is given in Hydes Relig. Vet. Perf. The *Zend a vesta*, or supposed writings of Zoroaster, were translated into French by M. Anquetil du Perron, and published at Paris, in 3 vols. 4to. 1771. The authenticity of this work was the subject of much controversy, and produced a confutation of it in the " *Lettre a M.A. du Perron, &c. Oct. Lond.* 1771", from Sir. W. Jones; who has, however, with much generosity, allowed considerable merit to his deceased antagonist, in a recent publication—Anniversary Dissertation on the Persians, 1789.

WHEN

When joined to *Alif*, as in the fecond *ha* of the laſt example, the fyllable appears as a double upright comma. See No. 71.—It is fometimes little more than a fmall turned ſtroke, as in *hemchunank*, No. 73; and it is often defcribed like a heart, as in the upper figure of *Hemeh*, all, No. 78; alfo in *Mihr*, the Sun*, No. 84; or as a circle with a ſtroke paſſed through it, as in *Beher*, to all, every, &c. the middle figure, No. 42; and it is often defcribed as a little circumflex: thus in *Hemeh*, all, the loweſt figure, No. 78; and in *Hemchu*, like as, fo, &c. No. 85.

It is frequently defcribed by an open turn of the pen, as in the word *Hind*, India, No. 38. Of initial *ha*, when expreſſed by a turned figure or circumflex, I ſhall here remark that it often is brought fo near to the lower part, or the whole fo rounded, as to aſſume, in fome inſtances, the appearance of the letter *Ssad*, irregularly expreſſed—(See under that letter) as in *hemchu*, like, as, &c. No. 85.

When medial connected, in *Talyk* MSS. *ha* is generally written as in the words *Bechefhm hai*, No. 16; and *Beher*, to all, every, &c. the upper figure, 42: but it fometimes does not defcend fo low on the line, as in the lower-moſt figure of the fame number.

* This word may be pronounced *mahur, moor,* &c. and has various fignifications accordingly; among others it means a gold coin, current in India, a feal, ring, love. See the note on *Aftaub*, in the next chapter.

MEDIAL

CHAP. II.]   PERSIAN MISCELLANIES.   39

MEDIAL connected *ha*, is sometimes expressed as the initial, thus in *Hey hat*, a vast desart, No. 86: when final, this letter is commonly described by a plain circle or figure of *Nought*, as in *Padishah*, a King, No. 13: and *Ghemzeh*, No. 44: this is the case when unconnected, and according to the *Niskhi* hand; but the Persians in their *Tàlick* manuscripts have deviated very much from the simplicity of that kind of writing, when this letter occurs in the end of a word, connected; for they frequently express it by a little curl of the pen: as in many of the foregoing examples, particularly *Auncheh*, No. 3: *Cheh*, No. 25: *Seyah*, No. 45: *Ashufteh*, No. 64: *Keh*, No. 72: *Wallah*, No. 77. No. 103, &c. &c. From these examples it will appear how very abruptly a final *ha* is joined, sometimes, to another letter; and in the lower figure, No. 39: *Sheh*, for *Shah*, a King, it is almost confounded with the stroke of *Shin*.

FINAL *ha* is sometimes irregularly joined to letters, which are so prolonged as to involve in the extremity of their flourish, the little *o*, or circle that expresses *ha**, as in *Mandeh*, remained, &c. No. 35: *Chehreh*, face, air, &c. No 36, and in *Anduh*, grief, &c. No. 37.

IN No. 78, three instances are given of initial and final *ha* in the word *Hemeh* all.

* Similar liberties have been taken by the Greek Scribes; thus in the combination (for it cannot be called a contraction) of the letters *ro* and *omikron*, in ῥοεω; of *ro* and *alpha* in ἀρϱαm.

To

40   PERSIAN MISCELLANIES.   [Chap. II.

To exprefs *ta*, and in the feminines of fome nouns, a final *ha*, with two points over, is frequently written as in the *Niſkhi* hand.

Of the letter Ya.

When initial or medial, this letter is known by its two diacritical points below, which diftinguifh its ftroke or body from B, P, T, N, &c. this body is fometimes rounded or lengthened at will, as in *Befiaur*, much, many, &c. No. 14: and *Shirauz*, the name of a city in Perfia, No. 49. In fome writings the medial connected *ya* is fcarcely marked, unlefs by its points; as in the word *Ameedum*, my hope, No. 12.

When placed before *Mim*, medial or final, it is often defcribed by a kind of curve or femicircular turn, but ftill known by its points below, as in *Solyman*, No. 47; and *Teflym*, No. 19: and in other combinations, as in *Seemeen*, filvered, of filver, &c. No. 87.

Of *Ya* final, the extremity is fometimes carried up ftraight and high, fo as to appear like a final *alif*, as in *Shuky*, jollity, mirth, &c. No. 26; and this ftroke is often brought fo clofe to the oppofite fide of the letter, as to inclofe nearly the whole fpace; thus in *Gohurhay*, jewels, No. 71.

It is fometimes on the contrary, much feparated, and the letter open at top, as in *Becheſkmhay*, to the eyes, &c. No.

CHAP. II.]   PERSIAN MISCELLANIES.   41

No. 16: But in all it is to be remarked that the firſt or right hand ſtroke is generally higher above the line than the other, as in moſt of the examples before quoted; and in the following ſpecimens.

As in the Arabian *Niſkhi* hand*, the tail of final *ya* is ſometimes turned back; thus (with points in the word *Sawky*, a cup-bearer, water-carrier, No. 88; and (without points) as in *Peſy*, many, more, &c. No. 54: From this circumſtance in many combinations, a word terminating as above, aſſumes frequently a very ſtrange appearance, as in *Geety*, the world, No. 20: where although the points of medial and final *ya* are marked, the whole ſeems irregular and confuſed.—For the points ſee next chapter.

FINAL *ya* unconnected, is ſometimes thrown above the other letters of a word, in a fanciful manner, as in *Sadi*, the name of a moſt celebrated Poet, No. 48; and the ſame word ſtill more irregularly written in No. 89.

AND it is often deſcribed as almoſt a ſtraight line, drawn horizontally over the other letters of a word, with ſcarcely any turn at the beginning (which is to be obſerved in *Sadi*, No. 48) as in *Pery-rooi*, with the face of an angel or fairy, No. 90. For ſome other irregularities in the poſition of final

---

* Je (ya) finale interdum retrocedit, &c.—See " Waſmuth. Arab. Gr. p. 3." and the Alphabetum Arabicum of the learned Erpenius prefixed to his hiſtory of the Patriarch Joſeph, from the Koran; 4to, 1617. Leyden.

G   *ya,*

ya, and difficulties occafioned by the omiffion or mifplacing of this letter's diacritical points, I refer the reader to the two fucceeding chapters and the engraved fpecimens.

Of LAM-ALIF.

IN the Arabic and Perfian Grammars, this compound character is generally placed at the end of the alphabet: it is, in fact, compofed of *Lam*, in the hollow of whofe curve or lower part, the letter *Alif* is inferted, as in the plain *Nifkhi* hand. But this *Alif* is fometimes placed upright, and not in the hollow of *Lam*, as *Gulaùb** Rofewater, No. 91; and it is often fo blended with the turn of *Lam* as to appear like part of that letter, as in the word *Laleh*, a tulip, No 92.

BUT of this character, as of all the others, many examples, will be given in the fucceeding fpecimens, and many irregularities and difficulties of combination explained, which

---

* So fond are the luxurious Perfians of the Rofe's delightful odour, that they not only fprinkle moft profufely in their apartments, the water diftilled from its leaves, but having prepared it with cinnamon and fugar, they infufe it with the coffee, which they drink. The Rofe of *Shirauz* is reckoned the moft excellent of the Eaft; and the effence of it highly efteemed even in the furtheft parts of India; the fcrapings of Sandal-wood are often added in diftillation to the leaves of this flower; but the pure effential oil, or thick fubftance, which they call ‎عطر گل *Ottar-gul*, or effence of Rofes, is more precious than gold.—See "Kœmpfer's Amenit. Exot:" 374; the remarks on Shirauz, in page 26, &c. of this Effay, and fome paffages in the fifth and fixth chapter.

have,

CHAP. II.]   PERSIAN MISCELLANIES.   43

have, I am well aware, efcaped me in this fuperficial analyfis of the alphabet; and as the chief difficulties and inaccuracies of Perfian writing are occafioned by the omiffion or falfe collocation of points, I have thrown together in the next chapter, fuch obfervations on them, as the perufal of feveral hundred original manufcripts has enabled me to make.

CHAPTER III.

OF THE DIACRITICAL POINTS.

IT is almost unneceſſary to inform the reader (ſuppoſed to be already acquainted with the *Niſkhi*, alphabet) that in the Arabic and Perſian languages the points conſtitute an eſſential part of the letters, and that according to their ſituation and number, they diſtinguiſh one character from another; thus a little ſtroke, with one point over, is an *N*; with two, a *T*; with one point under, a *B*, &c. In this reſpect they differ from the points in the Hebrew language, where they ſupply the place of vowels, and govern the ſenſe and pronunciation of words without affecting in the leaſt the characters of which thoſe letters are compoſed, as in the trite example דבר whoſe three letters continue invariably the ſame, whilſt the word, according to the nature and number of vowel-points applied to it, may be pronounced no leſs than eight different ways, *dabar*, *dobar*, *dibber*, &c. and the ſenſe accordingly changed*.

* See " Bayley's Entrance into the Sacred Language," p. x. Duod. Lond. 1732.

CHAP. III.]   PERSIAN MISCELLANIES.   45

THE importance of accuracy in the use of the Persian points is obvious, as any omission, confusion or misapplication of them may totally change the letters, and of course the words themselves. To such inaccuracies in rough copies, we may ascribe numberless errors, which, as I before said, (Chapter I.) have found their way into manuscripts very beautifully written, but which have been transcribed from those erroneous copies.

IN books, however, very correctly transcribed, it is not unusual to omit totally the diacritical points of final *ya*, the form of that letter, if properly expressed, securing it in general from any mistake—but when hastily written in some combinations, and its points omitted, final *ya*, has often, at first sight, the appearance of a final *sin*; thus in *Mahy*, a fish, No. 83; and I have seen the word *Shud*, was, described as in the upper figure No. 39; without its points: but such irregularity is rarely to be found in any manuscripts, except those written in the *Shekesteh* hand.

ALTHOUGH the just number of points may be expressed, yet they are often so irregularly placed and thrown together, as to require from the beginner a minute analysis, with study and time, as in the words, " *Aun aftaub eft*," that is the sun, No. 93 : here the point of *fa* is combined with those of medial *ta*, the *ba*, *sin*, and final *ta* are written over the first part of the word, and the point of *ba* placed at the end of all, nearly under the final *ta*. But the sense suggests the true letter, although the situation of that point gives to this cha-

racter

racter the appearance of a final *Ba*, and the final *ta*, being furnished with its points, shews that if any be placed under it, they must belong to some other letter of the word—a little consideration will, therefore, prove that the point placed irregularly under final *ta*, can belong to no other letter than the *ba*, of *aftaub*.

AND though of final *ya*, the points are often omitted, yet those of that letter, initial or medial, cannot be left out, without reducing the reader to the necessity of supplying the equivocal body of that character with imaginary points, according to his conception of the sense, thus in No. 94, by adding points above and below, the figure may be made to spell, *Sepeed*, *Sheneed*, and many other combinations.

HERE I shall observe that when two letters come together, whose points in Number are properly three, these generally affect the same mode of description, as the points over *Shin*, or under the letter *pa*, that is, as if within a triangle, or forming a kind of pyramid; thus in the word *Aftaub* *, the Sun,

---

* It may naturally be supposed, that the ancient Persians, to whom the sun was an object of religious veneration, had many names by which they expressed that glorious luminary. The name here given is one of those most generally used, and the word *Mihr*, (See note Chap. 2d) was principally applied to the sun as a sacred name. Of *Mihr* was compounded the name of *Mihridad*, whom Tacitus calls *Meherdates*, and the Greeks endeavouring to etain the aspiration in the first syllable, style *Mithridates*; in like manner they express the word *Mihr* by *Mithra*. According to a writer quoted by the learned *Selden* (*De Diis Syris-Moloch*) the Sun was also called in Persian *Adad*; and the celebrated Dr. Hyde, has enumerated many other epithets and titles, by which it was distinguished. See the Relig. Veter. Persarum."

No.

CHAP. III.] PERSIAN MISCELLANIES. 47

No. 17; alfo *Avftadeh* fallen, No. 22; and *Nutvan*, cannot, it is impoffible, &c. No. 95. Thefe are examples of letters whofe points are above the line: but when they are below, the bafe of the triangle, if I may ufe the expreffion, is to be next the line, or the pyramid reverfed; that is, two points parallel with the line, and one under, as this figure will beft explain.

SEE alfo *Biya*, come, ho! bring thou, &c. No. 97, *Peer*, old, an elder, &c. No. 98, and Nos. 17, 22, and 95, as above. Among fome hundred manufcripts which I have examined, there are but two in which this rule has not been obferved, and even in thofe books the deviations from it were very rare, although written throughout with much coarfenefs and inaccuracy. But the three points are often defcribed, having the two next the line, whether above it or below, blended together, as in *Shimfhad*, the box-tree, No. 11. *Imfheb*, this night, No. 52; and *Goft*, he faid, No. 62. Alfo, when below the line, as in *Afp*, a horfe, No. 18; *Pery-rooee*, fairy-faced, or beautiful, No. 90.

IN a Perfian manufcript now before me, very coarfely written, I obferve, that when the fame letter occurs twice in one word, the tranfcriber has expreffed the points belonging to thofe two letters, as if there was but one. Thus, in the word *Bulbul*,

48   PERSIAN MISCELLANIES.   [CHAP. III.

Bulbul, a nightingale*, one point below ferves for the two *ba's*, as in this figure,

Also, in the word *Shemſheer*, a ſcymetar, or ſword, where the points of one *Shin* are uſed for thoſe of both, and the word is thus written

THE points belonging to ſome ſingle characters are often expreſſed by a little curled ſtroke, as thoſe of *Shin* in *Kooſhteh*, ſlain, &c. No. 100, and *Shud*, was, No. 101 : of *Chim*, in the word *Chun*, when, like as, &c. No. 102 ; and in *Picheed*, for the infinitive *Picheedun*, to aſſociate with, to twiſt, involve, &c. No. 99. But it is not only when three points come together, that they are thus confuſed and blended; we find, in ſome manuſcripts, the two points of *ta, ya, kaf,* &c. expreſſed by a little figure, as in Nos. 86, 87, 88, and many others; and ſometimes ſcarcely more than a ſingle point to mark them, as in *aſt* or *eſt*, he is, &c. No. 4: *Daughy*, a wound or ſcar, No. 109.

THE two points belonging to ſome letters, are often placed one perpendicularly over the other: as in *Yſhk*, violent

---

* I have already mentioned this favourite of the Perſians, in the introduction, and ſhall have occaſion in the courſe of the following chapters, to quote ſome paſſages on the ſubject from the Eaſtern poets.

love,

Chap. III.]   PERSIAN MISCELLANIES.   49

love, No. 59: *Kumaunet**, thy bow, No. 70; and *Hekyket*, truth, reality, No. 63.

The points are not always placed exactly over or under the characters to which they belong, as the reader muſt have already perceived in many of the examples, particularly that of *Ba* in *Bokhara*† a City, No. 8; of *Ta* in *Grifty*, No. 21; of

* The word *Gumaun*, ſignifies an opinion, doubt, &c. and ſhould be written with three points over the firſt letter to diſtinguiſh it from *Kumaun*, a bow.—" Sed Scriptores nun-
" quam fere apponunt iſta tria puncta et ideo multoties oritur confuſio, quia multa
" nomina inter ſe diverſa ſcribuntur eodem modo, &c. &c."—See the old " Grammat.
" Linguæ Perſicæ," by Father Ignatius.—Rome, 1661, 4to p. 7; where he quotes the word in queſtion.

† Bokhara is the name of a celebrated city in Tranſoxania, or that country beyond the river *Gihoon*, which the Perſians alſo call the *Aub-i-Amù*, or waters of *Amù*; the city is ſurrounded by an immenſe wall, with ſeven gates, and contains a great number of handſome edifices; its gardens are watered by the river *Sogd*, whence the Province has been ſtyled *Sogdiana*; and it is celebrated as the birth place of many learned men, among whom *Avicenna* is the moſt eminent.—See the " Hiſt: Priorum Regum Pers: from Mirkond: of the ingenious Bernard de Ieniſch, 4to Vienna, 1782—p. 148—9: where he quotes that couplet from the Sonnet of Hafiz, ſo well known by the beautiful tranſlation of Sir Wm Jones.

" Sweet Maid if thou wouldſt charm my ſight,
" And bid theſe arms thy neck infold,
" That roſy cheek, that lily hand,
" Would give thy poet more delight
" Than all *Bokhara's* vaunted gold,
" Than all the gems of *Samarcand*."

See Jones Perſ. Grammar, p. 131, third edit. Lond. 1783, 4to; and his Aſiatic Poems and Tranſlations, p. 59, Octavo, Lond. 1777, Second Edition.

H   *Kha*

PERSIAN MISCELLANIES.   [CHAP. III.

Kha and *ya* in *Zelekha*, No. 27; of *fa*, in *Firmuden*, to command, No. 65; also in *Hezret*, majesty, &c. No. 57; where the point of *Zzad* is placed so much to the left of that letter as to seem belonging to the stroke of *ta* above it, which, if its own points had not been expressed, would thus become a final B: See also *Imsheb*, to night, No. 52.

Of the arbitrary manner of placing the points, frequent instances occur in the subjoined specimens: those of medial and final *ya* reversed, and of *ta*, in *Geety*, the world, No. 20. of *fa* and *ta* in *Grifty*, No. 21: In the words " *Az andisheh dilesh*, from the anxiety or thoughts of his heart, No. 103,— the points of medial *Shin* in *Andisheh*, and of final *Shin*, in *Dilesh*, are placed over the dash of the latter; and those of *ya* in *Andisheh*, under the middle of the body or dash of *Shin* in that word. The points are often placed so high above their letter, as to seem rather belonging to an upper line, or some other word, especially when the body of the letter is not strongly marked, as in *Auncheh*, No. 3: *Zeleekha*, No. 27; and the same irregularity may be found, when the points are below the line.

The stroke of some other letter often intervenes between the diacritical points, and the letter to which they belong; as in *Sadi*, No. 48, where the three first letters are between the final *ya* and its points; and in *Aunkeh*, he who, No. 104: where the point of *Nun* is thrown above the stroke of *Caf*,

also

CHAP. III.]   PERSIAN MISCELLANIES.   51

alſo in *Bazy*, play, ſport, &c. No. 105, where the final *ya* reverſed is between the point and the body of the letter *za*, and the points of *ya*, are placed to the left.

A point is ſometimes ſo irregularly placed as to ſeem touching a letter to which it does not properly belong; as in the word *Khauk*, earth, clay, &c. No. 106: and in *Deſt a Sadi*, No. 107, the hand of Sadi, where the points of final *ta* in the firſt word, being deſcribed as blended together, are placed touching the ſtroke of the letter *ſin* in *Sadi*.

WHEN *ya* is the final letter of a word, and expreſſed by an irregular flouriſh (ſee under *ya* laſt chapter), the letter immediately preceding and connected with it, may be known by the ſituation of its point, if it be one of thoſe letters which poſſeſs ſuch a characteriſtic; for if the point be to the right, it is a *ba*, or ſome letter whoſe points are below the line, as in *Javabi*, an anſwer, No. 108.

IF the point, be at the left, it belongs to one of thoſe letters, whoſe point or points, we deſcribe above the line, as in *Daughy* a mark, wound, ſcar, &c. No. 109; and in *Mani*, No. 110, the name of a famous Perſian painter, and Hereſiarch, who is called in our Eccleſiaſtical hiſtory *Manes*, and his followers *Manicheans*. By the Perſians he is ſtyled " *Mani Nakhaſh*," or " the painter*."   THE

---

* Of this ancient Artiſt's paintings, ſo celebrated by the Poet *Nezami*, no veſtiges have been diſcovered: equally an object of religious perſecution to the Chriſtian and Mahometan

H 2

THE points in writings where the characters are large and clearly expressed, are not always round, but rather a kind of square, or lozenge.

I shall close this chapter by observing, that it is not unusual in many finely written MSS. to decorate some parts of a page, particularly ornamented writings, with a figure like that of three points, as in plate V. No. 5—But a little attention and habit will tell when those points are merely ornamental, and consequently superfluous.

metan Zealots, it can hardly be supposed that the works of this arch heretic would descend to the present day, through fifteen centuries, without any other injuries than those of time.—That they have totally perished is most probable: but that all the traditions concerning this impostor's skill in painting, are mere fictions, is an opinion I would not, by any means, hastily adopt, notwithstanding the gross anachronism, by which *Nazami* has introduced him into his history of Alexander, as contemporary with the Macedonian Prince. On the probable nature of those pictures, with which he is said to have decorated his *Enghelioon*, or gospel, and *Arzhenk*, his book or collection of drawings so often alluded to by Persian writers, I shall offer some observations in another place.

CHAPTER

CHAPTER IV.

MISCELLANEOUS OBSERVATIONS.

FROM the confused collocation of letters, and the irregular position or omission of points, we find in many *Talik* manuscripts, that not only whole sentences and lines, but also single words assume a very fantastic and uncommon appearance: as in the word *Hasyl*, gain, result, &c, No. 111: where the top *Alif* joins the lower part of the letter *Ssad*.

ALSO in *Dilfereeb*, alluring or charming the heart, No. 112, where the point of final *ba*, is most irregularly placed under the letter *Lam*, and the *ya* and final *ba*, thrown over the other letters, so that the point of *fa* seems to belong to the stroke of *ba, ya,* and the points of *ya,* are placed under the letter *Lam*.

OF a letter intervening between the points of another, and its proper body, some instances have been given in the last chapter, particularly No. 48 in *Sadi*: *Aunkeh*, No. 104; and the word *Bazy*, No. 105; from this circumstance, and the placing of *Kafs*, two points to the left, instead of over their proper character, the word *Caf*, No. 113, appears at first sight

54   PERSIAN MISCELLANIES.   [Chap. IV.

fight a little difficult: It is the name of a fabulous mountain much celebrated in the Eastern Romances*.

From the nature of some letters, which hang from, or depend on each other in certain combinations, a word often seems nearly upright, or perpendicular, as in *Hemchu*, like as, so, &c. No. 85.

To fill up a space, and render all the lines of equal length, which the Persians much affect, particularly in writing poetry, they often divide or prolong a word in a very fanciful manner: thus in *Hekayety* a story, history, &c. No. 114; where a space is left between the syllables *heka* and *yety*, under which is drawn the reversed tail of final *ya*: and for the same purpose they often connect two letters by a long dash or flourish of the pen, which has in many instances the appearance of the letter *sin* as usually written in the *Talik* hand; thus in *Heech*, nothing,

---

* The mountain of Câf (which some suppose mount Tauris) is said to be the residence of a fabulous animal, an immense bird or Griffin called the *Simurgh*; there, notwithstanding the proverbial barrenness of this dreary mountain, the voracious monster is enabled to satisfy the calls of hunger; so great is the liberality of heaven to all its creatures. "The " Omnipotent," (says *Sadi*) spreadeth his table to such an extent, that even the Simurgh, in " the mountain of Câf, eateth his share." The original Persian lines are given in the " Asiatic Miscellany," No. 2, p. 242, Calcutta, 1789, 4to. and are as follows:—
    " Chenaun pihen khân kerm kesterd
    " Keh Simoorgh der Kaf kesimet khcord."
In my manuscript copy of the *Bostan*, (one which the celebrated Chardin brought from Persia,) instead of *Kesimet*, I find the word *Roozee*, which we may translate, a daily allowance, from *Rooz*, a day.

no,

CHAP. IV.] PERSIAN MISCELLANIES. 55

no, never, &c. No. 115; where the final *Chim* has but one point, (See under that letter, Chap. II.) and in the word *Muheyia*, arranged, prepared, &c. No. 116: where a long dafh connects the *ya* with final *Alif.*

IN the words *Bi-hafyl*, thus written, [Arabic] (compounded of *bi* or *bee*, without, and *hazyl*, gain, refult, advantage,) the *ya* which fhould be final in the firft word, is irregularly joined to the *hha* of the next, and its points placed with the point of *ba*, while a long dafh connects the *hha* with *Alif* in *Hazyl*.

AND they fometimes fill up a line with little oblique ftrokes, as in Plate V. No. 6.

BUT on the other hand, when a line is crowded they often blend letters fo as to create much feeming confufion; thus in the words *Ghemmà Yfhk* the pain or affliction of love, No. 117; the body of *Ghain* is made to ferve alfo for that of *ain* which begins the word *Yfhk*, love: the point above, which conftituted that character *Ghain*, being in imagination done away.

IN the word *Padfhah*, a king, the *alif* and *dal* are irregularly joined at the top, (as thofe of *Shim Shad*, already mentioned, No. 11; Chap. II. Letter *Dal*) and the ftroke of *Shin* in *Shah*, is brought through the former fyllable *Pad*, which circumftance, with the abfence of *fhin's* diacratical points, gives the word a confufed appearance, thus, [Arabic]

IT

It is sometimes considered as ornamental to bring the flourish of one letter so far round as to touch that of another, though belonging to a different word, as in *Keshty Noah**, the ship or ark of Noah, No. 118; where the tail of final *ya*, in the first word, is joined to that of final *hha* in *Noah*.

In the words *Shudy gunge*, thou wert a treasure, No. 119; the flourish of final *ya* in *Shudy*, not only touches, but is quite blended into the curve or tail of the final *jim* in *Gung* or *Gunj*, the point of *jim* is therefore placed in the hollow of that flourish, which constitutes final *ya*, and the points of this letter are altogether omitted, which circumstance increases the seeming difficulty of the whole combination.

As the Persians scarcely ever divide a word, by placing its parts in different lines, when too much crowded, they invariably write such parts of words above the line, never below, as in *Aumedeſt*, No. 9; *Sâdi*, No. 48; *Laſhkureſh*, No. 50; *Hezeret*, No. 57; *Aun aftaubeſt*, No. 93; and many others.

The name of *Sadi* having occurred three or four times in the course of this work, I shall here take occasion to mention, that the birth of this celebrated poet, happened at Shirauz, in the year of our Æra 1175; he was author of the *Guliſtan*, or

---

* The story of Noah is related in the Koran, (of which the Seventy-first Chapter bears his name) but the Mahomedans have taken some liberties with the original narrative. The Ark, according to a Mufulman commentator, was twelve hundred cubits long, and six hundred broad. See " Savary's Coran, Vol. I. 245. Note, chapter of Hod.

حکایت بیست و ششم نفست از شیخ ابوصر سلامه غبداوی خوانند
که کوشش بنود ماه ذوالقعده وکه و فتن در فریه شیخ مطابا وزرای رضی آمنه
جدا وعظیم یعنی ملخ بسیار میکند پشت جند آنکه تمام پوشیده
بود و مقدم ایشان مردی بود بسوار بر یک جد آباد و ایسگفت لا اله الا الله
محمد رسول الله کل نعمة من الله مرحا جانب که امر و نوحه میکرد و ملخ و پخال ا د
میرفت بعد از آن شیخ مطابا وزرای در صحن برآ و به خود سر و ن آمد و ندا
کرد یا جنود الله ارجعی من جهنا و رحال آن ملخ همه بازگشتند وانه انبوه
مجموعاً پیش شیخ افنا شیخ فرمود امر دارا که خراجه باعث شرک یغیر
اذن سپاه پس کشتی امرد درهای شیخ افنا وادی ابی سپیده وعذر
میخواست و استغفار میکرد تا اینکه شیخ خشنود شند وانجا ز و سلب کرده
بو دبا زداد فرمود بمیر و بر و درحال امر د با زور بوا پر به در فت بمو تنر
دار ملخ در طا و عراق افنا و خلقی انزا گرشتند و قوت خود می ساختند

CHAP. IV.]   PERSIAN MISCELLANIES.   57

Bed of Roses; the *Bostan*, or Fruit Garden; the *Molammàt*, or Rays of Light, and a large collection of odes and sonnets, alphabetically arranged in a *Divàn*. The first of these works has been published with a Latin version by the learned Gentius*; in the German language by Olearius†; and by another person in French‡. Of the second, some partial extracts have appeared in the Asiatic Miscellany‖. The third, is a manuscript extremely scarce, and from the *Divaun*, which contains above a thousand beautiful poems, very few passages have yet found their way into print. Sadi was the author of fourteen or fifteen other works; but Mr. Le Bruyn, (see his Travels) must have been misinformed, when he learned, on visiting the poet's tomb in 1705, that twenty Arabic volumes were still extant of his composition. I shall not here suppress, that there is also attributed to *Sadi*, (although I hope without foundation) a small

---

* Rosarium Politicum, &c. Amsterdam, 1651. Folio, Persian and Latin.
(Saadi) Rosarium Politicum, cura Gentii. Amsterdam, 1655. Duodecimo. Latin.
† Persianischer Rosenthal ubersetzet von A. Olearius, with plates. Schlefwig. 1654. Folio.
‡ This French version, which was probably made from the Latin or German translation before mentioned, is entitled, " Gulistan ou L'Empire des Roses, Traité des Mœurs des Rois; composé par Musladini Saadi, Prince des Poetes Persiens, Traduit du Persan, par M. ***. Paris. 1737. Duodecimo.
‖ Asiatic Miscellany, No. 2, p. 235, &c. Calcutta, 1789, Quarto, where part of the preface to, and a passage from the *Bostan* are given; of this work, some translations into French may be found in the travels of the Chevalier Chardin.

I   collection

collection of short poetical compositions (see page 19,) inculcating lessons of the grossest sensuality, and breathing all the licentiousness of the most unchaste imagination. These in the manuscripts before me are inconsistently placed among the beautiful, moral, and sentimental distichs which follow our author's *Divan*; and in an Arabic introduction, he declares his repentance of having composed those indelicate verses, which, however, he excuses on account of their giving a relish to the other poems, " as salt is used in the seasoning of meat :" and if one can allow any merit to such productions, it may be said of him as of Petronius, " that he wrote the most impure things " in the purest language*."

An ingenious friend, whom I shall mention in the course of this Essay, when on the subject of eastern music, is in possession of a most valuable manuscript Treatise on that art, which from many circumstances he conjectures to be the work of *Sadi*; the language is Persian, and the subject treated in a scientific and masterly manner. Of this celebrated poet, the portrait was lately to be seen in a building near *Shirauz*,

---

* Since this passage was written, I have had an opportunity of inspecting the first volume of *Sadi's works* (printed at Calcutta in folio, 1791 : in Persian, with an English preface, &c. by J. H. Harrington, Esq.) sent as a valuable present from Sir W. Jones, to the late Professor Schultens, in whose Library at Leyden, I was permitted to examine it: and I was sorry to find, that in the list there given of Sadi's works, the " *Book of Impurities*," is enumerated as authentic.

representing

CHAP. IV.]   PERSIAN MISCELLANIES.   59

reprefenting him as a venerable old man, with a long filver beard and flowing robes, holding in his right hand a crooked ivory ftaff, and in the other a charger of incenfe*. He lived to the advanced age of one hundred and fixteen, and his tomb is ftill vifited with the refpect due to claffic ground, at a little diftance from Shirauz, his native city.

BUT I return to my fubject: it is not only parts of words that are thus placed above the line, fometimes two or three entire words are written over the former part of it. In the courfe of the annexed fpecimens, many inftances are given of the confufion arifing from this circumftance: but I fhall here give a few examples of irregularities in the collocation of letters and words from manufcripts immediately before me.

IN the word *Gulaub*, Rofewater, No. 91: final *Ba* is above the line, its ftroke touching the *Lam-Alif*, and its point below, under the juncture of *Gaf* and *Lam*.

IN *Kafhgy*, would to heaven! &c. No. 120; the two firft letters, *Caf* and *Alif* are placed within the ftroke of *Shin* above, and the reverfed tail of final *ya* below: which hangs from the medial *Gaf* by a ftrange turn of the pen.

IN the compound word *Dilruba*, ravifher of hearts, &c. No. 121, the *ra* and *vaw* are over the hook of *Lam*, and the

---

* See "Francklin's Tour from Bengal to Perfia, in the years 1786-87, p. 97, Octave, London, 1790.

I 2   turn

turn of *Ba* touches its extremity: the point of *ba* is thrown to the left of the word.

In the words " *Por Kurdeh az aub,*" filled with water, No. 122: the final *ba* is thrown over the other letters, and its point placed at the left extremity of all: whilſt the orthographical mark *Medda*, belonging to the word *aub*, is placed over the ſtroke of final *ba*, and increaſes the confuſion by appearing, in ſome reſpects, like another letter.

But it ſometimes happens that in poetry, where the line is crowded towards the end, not only one row of letters or words is placed above the line, but frequently a third over the ſecond, ſo as to form a very odd appearance, and not unfrequently create much confuſion and difficulty: But one muſt always read upwards, beginning with the loweſt line: as will be proved in ſome of the engraved ſpecimens, and explained in the following chapters.

In " *Herkes Sheneedy,*" every one heard, or was hearing, &c., No. 123, we find the words and letters aſcend even to the fourth degree: the *Ha* and *Ra* are connected by a long daſh; ſuch as already has been mentioned; the word *Kefs* is over them, and the two ſyllables " *Sheneed,*" over that; the final *ya* of *Sheneedy* is above all; the points of medial *ya*, (which, as I before ſaid, Chap. III. cannot be omitted) are placed in the hook of the letter *Sin*: and thoſe of *final ya* are not expreſſed.

CHAP. IV.]   PERSIAN MISCELLANIES.   61

IN the words *Jaumee-Shraub*, a cup of wine, No. 124: the letters *Shin* and *Ra* touch the upper parts of *Alif* and final *Mim* in *Jaum*: the *Alif* of *Shraub* is placed by itself over the *Shr*, and still above that is the body of final *Ba*, touching the top of *Alif*: its point thrown under the left extremity.

EVEN the letters of a single word are thus placed above each other in many manuscripts, as in *Dildar*, a sweet heart, a mistress, &c. No. 125: where the first *D* is by itself on the lowest line; *L* and connected *D*, on the second line, *Alif* over them, and above all the last letter *Ra*.

FROM this circumstance it sometimes happens that the highest letter almost touches or seems to belong to the line above, and in other situations it is not unusual to run the stroke of some letters so high as to unite with that of another letter belonging to the line above. An instance of this occurs in a manuscript before me where the word *Keshty*, a Ship, &c. is joined by the prolonged stroke of the letter *Gaf*, to the tail of *Ra* in *birun*, out, &c. a word belonging to an upper-line. See No. 126.

FROM the improper connection of two words, by making initial or medial letters which should be final, or similar false combinations, some confusion frequently arises, as in the words " *Dur een wakt*," in this season, at this time, &c. No. 127; where the *N* of *een* (for *aeen*, with *Alif*) which ought to be

final

62   PERSIAN MISCELLANIES.   [CHAP. IV.

final, is defcribed as medial 'and connected with the *Vaw* of *Wakt*.

ALSO in *Aun zemeen*, that land or country, No. 128; where, in like manner, the *N* of *aun*, which fhould be final, is initial, and connected with the *Za* of *Zemeen*. In the word *Kheyal*, No. 96, we find the *Alif* joined to the *Lam*, improperly, by a ftroke from the top of the former.

IN fome books, it is much affected to defcribe the ftrokes or flourifhes of many letters as parallel with one another: thus, in the words *Muger Keh*, unlefs that, &c. No. 129; and in the fame number, *Gur Kurd*, if he makes, does, &c. Alfo in No. 130; *Az amber Serifhteh*, formed or compofed of ambergris*, (fpelt *anbr*) where the point of *Nun* is above the ftroke of *Sin* in *Serifhteh*, and the point of *Ba* under the long dafh which unites *Ba* with *Ra*: to this dafh is defcribed as parallel the ftroke of *Sin*.

AND the reader will find another example in the words " *Ez andifhefh dilefh*," before quoted, No. 103; And in *Nakafh*,

---

* Of mufk, camphire, ambergris, and fimilar fragrant fubftances, the Perfians believe angels to be formed, and other creatures endued with uncommon purity of nature; thus the poets compliment their miftreffes on the delightful odours which they diffufe; the aerial beings called *Peries*, are fuppofed to exift on perfumes alone; and even of Paradife, celeftial fragrance is among the chief delights! The wine which the faithful are there to be indulged with, is fealed with mufk; and fome authors affirm, that fhould the lovely Houries but fuffer one drop of their ambrofial fpittle to fall upon this earth, no human fenfe could bear the exquifite poignancy of its perfume.

painting,

CHAP. IV.]   PERSIAN MISCELLANIES.   63

painting, &c. following a word which ends in *Shin*, I have seen the strokes laid parallel, and the points situated as in No. 131; where the three first points, (to the right) are those of *Nun* and *Kaf* in *Nakash*. The three points in the middle, are those of the lower *Shin*, belonging to some preceding word: and the three points at the left of all, are those of final *Shin* in *Nakash*. Also in the word *Nedeedeh*, not seen, &c. No. 132, the *ya* and *dal* are placed over the *nun* and *dal* of the former syllable.

THE stroke of one letter is not unfrequently crossed through that of another, as in *Lashkuresh*, his army, No. 50; where *Caf* crosses the stroke of *Shin* final.

ALSO in the word "*Bergirift*," he takes up, &c. No. 133; where the stroke of *Gaf* crosses the *fa* and *ta* final above. In the word *Grift*, before quoted, No. 74, the stroke of *Gaf* reaches, but does not cross the *fa* or *ta*.

IT is not unusual, to place in the hollow of letters, which possess a large curve or sweep, some others of the word or sentence; as *Dureegh*, alas! No. 134; where *D* and *R* are in the hollow of final *Ghain*, and the points of the letter *ya*, irregularly thrown below.

IN *Dilruba*, before mentioned, No. 121; the *Ra* and *Vaw* are in the hook of *Lam*; and in *Nakash*, above quoted, No. 131, the curve of one final *Shin* is placed within that of another.

IN the words *Yek Guftar*, one saying, speech, conversation, &c. No. 135; the letters *Gfta*, of the second word are written within

within the hook of the preceding *Caf* of *Yek*; the *R* of *Guftar* placed so as to appear part of the first word.

In No. 80, before quoted, the final *Nun* of *Chun*, contains that of the second word *Men*.

I BEFORE observed (in the second Chapter under the respective letters) that in many manuscripts, the letters *Dal*, *Ra*, and *Vaw*, are hastily written, and may be often, at first sight, mistaken one for another: it accordingly happens that from the accidental concurrence of words, principally composed of these letters, and the neglect of a proper distance between the words, some very strange and confused appearances result: we will, for example, suppose the words " *Ora door awurd az doo rud*," to be negligently written as in No. 136; where the confusion occasioned by the resemblance of the letters *R*, *D*, and *Vaw*, is increased by the turning of the lower part of unconnected *Alif*. (See that letter in the second Chapter.)

The same difficulty arises from the same cause in reading Hebrew; and many serious mistakes have been occasioned by the resemblance of the letters *Beth* and *Caph*, *Daleth* and *Resh*, &c.*

AND here I shall remark, that many letters of the Arabic alphabet, still retain, in some measure, the form of their originals in the parent Hebrew: we can easily trace the *Daleth* in

* Consult the various works of the learned Bochart, Hyde, Lud: de Dieu, Pere Simon, and others.

the

the more curved body of *Dal*: the fame nearly of *Reſh* and *Ra*: and the *Zain* as in the *Vaw*, with its broad head, has fuffered very little alteration; and the three teeth of *Sin* and *Shin*, have only funk into the indentures of the correfponding letters which bear the fame names in the *Niſkhi* alphabet: But this remark encroaches on the department of the Arabian Antiquary, and I return to my fubject, the Graphical difficulties of Perfian manufcripts.

In many fine writings, where feveral letters are expreffed by mere hair-ftrokes, fome combinations produce a very confufed appearance, as in the words " *Gulzar-e-Irem**," the Rofe-bower, or garden of Irem, No. 137, where the point of *Za* touches the top of *Lam*, and the grammatical mark, which fhews the former of two fubftantives to govern a genitive cafe, is placed between the words *Gulzar*† and *Irem*; and being like the letters *Ra* and *Alif*, expreffed by a fine hair-ftroke, occafions fome confufion in the appearance of the whole.

---

* This garden or paradife of *Irem*, is frequently alluded to by the Mahometan poets; it is faid to have been planted in Arabia Felix, by an ancient and very impious king, whom Mohammed in the Koran, fpeaks of with horror; this prince, wifhing to be regarded as more than mortal, introduced all thofe who refpected him as a Divinity, into this terreftrial paradife, where they enjoyed all that was delicious and capable of gratifying the fenfes.— See D'Herbelòt Bibl. Orient. art. Iram.

† This mark gives the found of *e* or *i* fhort, and anfwers to the *Cafra* of the Arabs.— See Jones's Perfian Grammar, p. 10 and 18, and Richardfon's Arabic Ditto, p. 12.

Also in the words "*Buzruk gurdaniden*," to caufe to become great, large, &c. No. 138; in which example the point of *Za* almoſt touches the oblique ſtroke of *Caf*, which is feparated from its perpendicular one; (fee Letter *Gaf*, or *Caf*, Chap. II.) and within its hook or hollow, the *GRD* of the fecond word *Gerdaniden* are placed: the *Alif* of this word under the *Nyd*, the points of *ya* being thrown under the *Alif*, and the final *Nun* above all.

As in fome Arabic manufcripts, although the abfence of points fufficiently diftinguifhes fuch letters as *Hha*, *Sin*, *Ra*, &c. yet the writer frequently places over thefe characters certain marks which denote that the abfence of the points is not occafioned by his inaccuracy*: So in the Perfian word *Beroon*, out, No. 139; left it fhould be thought that over the long dafh between *ya* and *ra* any points ought properly to have been placed, a little mark or character is ufed for the fame purpofe as thofe above-mentioned in the Arabic writings: but as the moſt excellent Grammarian Erpenius obferves, fuch marks are feldom ufed in modern writings, and to be found only in manufcripts moſt accurately written†.—Of this defcription, indeed, is the manufcript from which the example is

---

* See, " Erpenius's Arabic Grammar," p. 7. 4to, 1636.—" Wafmuth's ditto, p. 3.— and " Walton's" ingenious " Introductio ad lectionem linguarum Orientalium," p. 61, Duodecimo. London, 1655.

† " Hæc tamen hodie rarò et non nifi in accuratiſſimè Scriptis obfervantur."—Erpenii Gram. Arab. 7.

given:

CHAP. IV.] PERSIAN MISCELLANIES. 67

given: a beautiful copy of the celebrated Romance by the Poet *Jaumi*, intitled the " Loves of Joseph and Zeleekha"

FROM the carelessness of the writer, should any letters be forgotten or omitted, they are generally supplied either over or under the line, as near as possible to their proper places: thus in the phrase, " *Chè arzoo daree?*"—what desire hast thou? what do you want? &c. No. 140, in which the *Ra* and *za* of *arzoo* were forgotten, and afterwards written below the line, the point of *za* being placed above it; and the *Ra* of *Daree*, which had been omitted, is placed above the line, and over the *Alif* of that word.

MISTAKES are sometimes corrected as with us in hastily written manuscripts, by drawing several strokes acrofs the erroneous word or paffage, and referring by a mark (as given in Plate V. No. 1) to the margin, where the word or paffage in question is correctly written.

OF two nouns substantive, the former governing a genitive cafe, is generally marked in well-written books, by the Arabic mark *Kefra* or *Cafra*, and known in pronunciation by a short kind of found which may be expreffed as *a* quick, *e* or *ee* or *ei* short*; as in *Gulzar-e-Irem*, before quoted, No. 137:

* Sir Wm Jones (Perf. Gram. p. 18) calls this *Kefra* a short *e*.—Mr Hadley in the Introduction to his Perfian Vocabulary, page 17; expreffes it by *ee* or *ei*;—and Mr Richardfon, in the preface to his Dictionary, second vol. p. vi. feems to give the preference to *a* short; there are cafes, I believe, in which it is beft written by *i* short.

K 2   *Deft-a-Sâdi*,

68   PERSIAN MISCELLANIES.   [CHAP. IV.

Deft-a-Sâdi, the hand of Sadi, No. 107; and in the line given in Plate VII. No. 1 : in the words *Jaiab-i-Skander*, the anfwer of Alexander: as the reader will find explained in the fixth chapter.

WHEN two words come together compofed of the fame letters, but whofe vowel-points are different, and confequently their meanings, it is ufual in well-written manufcripts to mark the vowel points, and thereby affift in afcertaining the fenfe: for the three letters *DRD*, with *Fatha*, pronounced *Derd*, fignify grief, pain, affliction, &c. The fame letters marked with the vowel-point *Damma*, are pronounced *Durd*, and mean dregs, fediment, &c. I have chofen thefe words for an example becaufe they occur in the engraved Specimen (frontifpiece,) laft line, the explanation of which the reader will find in the laft chapter.

CHARACTERS anfwering to our periods, commas, full ftops, &c. are unknown in Perfian writings : the end of a line in verfe, is fometimes marked, even though the fenfe be not complete, by little figures, of which, examples are given in the following plates. But in profe, efpecially where the fentence is quite finifhed, and a new fubject perhaps commenced, no orthographical mark, or other character, is ufed to afcertain the fenfe, but the words probably are crowded on each other. To this general remark, however, I have met with one or two exceptions, which will be found in the explanation of Plate V.

No.

CHAP. IV.]   PERSIAN MISCELLANIES.   69

No. 6; and No. 7, Chapter V. In the former number of which examples, the abrupt fenfe is marked by two little points or ftrokes; in the latter, by a vacant fpace left between the fentences.

THE word *Allah*, GOD, and other Arabic words or fentences, occurring in Perfian MSS. are frequently marked by their vowel points, and it is to be obferved, that quotations from the Koran*, or other ferious works in the Arabian language, are not only in general diftinguifhed by their vowel-points and orthographical characters, but affect a more upright and fquare appearance than the Perfian *Tálik* hand, and fometimes are written in the original *Nifkhi*.

* It feems undecided among European writers, whether the article *al*, in Arabic, prefixed to the word *Koran* or *Coran*, fhould in our tranflations be omitted as redundant after the Englifh article, or whether it fhould be retained and ufed with that, according to the practice of Herbelôt, and other eminent Orientalifts. Of this latter opinion, moft of our modern Englifh writers feem to be; yet, although I own, that from habit, both the eye and ear decide in favour of the article, and that in Latin, it may be ufed with elegance, I agree with thofe Orientalifts who fupprefs it, the fenfe being perfectly complete without this repetition of the article. I was of this opinion long before I knew that it was fupported by Monfieur Savary, who, in the preface to his French tranflation of the work in queftion, explains his reafon for adopting it. Although cuftom had authorized and rendered familiar the ufe of the *al*, yet being a grammatical impropriety, he fuppreffed it, and thinking it never too late to diveft one's felf of ill founded prejudices, he writes the word, *Coran*. " Perfuadè qu'il eft toujours temps de s'affranchir du joug d'un ufage mal-etabli j'ai ecrit, *le Coran*." Savary's Coran, 2 vols. Duodecimo. Amft. 1786. Page V.

PERSIAN MISCELLANIES. [CHAP. IV.

OF the numerical figures and their various combinations into hundreds and thousands, I shall say but little; Sir William Jones, in his most admirable Grammar, p. 91, having rendered any remarks by me on that subject unneceffary. I have given in Plate V. No. 8; the Persian figures as written in a fair manuscript before me, becaufe fome little difference of form appears in them, particularly the 4 and 5, from thofe in the Grammar; and I shall only remark, that in moft writings, where the word *Seh*, three, is expreffed by letters, it is ufual to place over the stroke of *Sin*, the numerical figure of 3, thus:

MARKS of reference and characters, diftinguishing poetry, are generally written in red ink; the moft common are given in Plate V. No. 1; and explained in the next chapter.

BY afcertaining the number of pages in a Perfian book, and counting the lines in any one page, it is eafy to difcover the exact number of lines contained in the whole volume, as every page (except perhaps the firft and laft) is ruled with an equal number.

A CATCH-WORD at the bottom of the right-hand page, generally leads the reader to the beginning of the left, and this catch-word is often written obliquely, as in the engraved fpecimen, (Frontifpiece,) fee Chapter VII.

THE pages are frequently ruled with golden lines, blue or red ink, &c. Verfes are generally written in two columns, as defcribed in Sir William Jones's Grammar, 146; each couplet being

CHAP. IV.]   PERSIAN MISCELLANIES.   71

being divided equally, and each member of a couplet forming part of a column, as will appear in some of the specimens annexed ; but two rows of couplets, that is, four columns, are found in many MSS. and each column, whether the page contains four, or only two, is generally separated from the next, by blue, red, or golden lines. The strokes of some letters are often found to exceed or encroach upon those lines, an instance is given in Plate VII. No. 5; Plate VIII. No. 1; and the Frontispiece.

VERSES in four columns are to be read in the following order, from right to left :

<u>   4   </u>   <u>   3   </u>   <u>   2   </u>   <u>   1   </u>

IN some cases, such as a marginal quotation, want of room, &c. a distich or tetrastich, is often written, as with us, one line or member of a couplet over the other.

THE transcribers generally conclude their work with the words, " *Tummet tummam al kittaub*, &c." " the book is com-
" pletely finished," frequently adding the author's name, with benedictions, the *taurich*,* or date, and often the titles of the

* Like the books printed among us in the early ages of the typographical art, the day and name of the month are often mentioned, and in some MSS. even the hour of the day or night on which the writing was finished, a custom probably borrowed from the Arabs, (see Casiri's Bibl: Arab: Hispana: Vol. I. pref. 7. Folio. 1760,) and perhaps from those *Hispano-Arabic* authors, the practice of placing at the end of books, the date and printer's name, &c. was first introduced into Europe.

reigning

reigning prince; sometimes to fill up the last page, they place the letters, *ta* and *mim*, (forming the Arabic word *Tumma*, which is the same as *Finis*, or the end) in this manner:

not unfrequently omitting, as in the present example, the diacritical points of *ta*.

But as the various combinations and contractions of letters, their irregularities, and graphical difficulties, are merely the subject of this work, and exactly the same, whether comprised in one, two, or four columns, in lines oblique or horizontal, ornamented or plain, I shall not swell this volume to an unnecessary bulk, by a multiplicity of examples; but proceed in the next chapter to explain the engraved specimens, which will best illustrate the observations here miscellaneously thrown together.

CHAPTER

162			161
بسم الله الرحمن الرحيم	ب ت ث	ج ح خ	ا
	د ذ	ر ز	
	س ش	ص ض	
	ط ظ	ع غ	
	ف ق	ك ل	
	م ن	و ه	ی

163

نشستن سلطان سکندر برتخت پادشاهی پی ی هـ پدر خود

164

جنگ کردن رستم با سهراب و کشته شدن سهراب از دست رستم

165

بجواب آمدن یوسیف علیه السلام زلیخا را نوبت دوم و نامه و تنقام وی د نشستن و بعقل و سوسن باز آمدن

166	167	
مثل تو نديده ام بديم	مانند تو آدمي در آفاق	اسكن نبود پري نبيم

169	168									
	1	2	3	4	5	6	7	8	9	10
	۱	۲	۳	۴	۵	۶	۷	۸	۹	۱۰
An. Messiæ				1798 — 1794						
An. Hegiræ				1209 — 1209						

CHAPTER V.

EXPLANATION OF THE MISCELLANEOUS SPECIMENS.

PLATE V. No. 1.

THE feven upper characters in this number, and others which the reader will foon become acquainted with, are ufed as marks of reference or diftinction, and the explanation of the paffage referred to is generally found between the lines, or in the margin.

THE four figures in the third line are moft commonly written in red ink, and denote that a paffage in verfe is immediately to follow: of this an example is given in the next plate. The loweft figures of this number are ufed, even in books of profe, to fill up a line, left a blank fpace fhould hurt the eye, and deftroy the uniformity of the writing.

PLATE V. No. 2.

" *Bifmillahi 'a'rrahiman' ar'raheem,*" " *In the name of God, the clement, and the merciful.*" This fentence, although Arabic, is prefixed to almoft every book in the Perfian language, whatever the fubject of it may be; it is the commencement of the *Fateha*, or opening chapter of the Koran, and is placed at the head

head of every other *Suret* or chapter of that work, except one.* In this sentence it is to be remarked, that the particle *b*, *in*, expels the *Alif* of the word *Ism*, " a name," and that the letter *Sin*, in that word, is prolonged by a long dash connecting it with *b*, and the final *Mim*. In this sentence alone, the *Alif* of *Ism* suffers an elision: in any other it should be expressed†. According to the original orthography, this sentence would be thus written:

" *Bsm allh alr-hhmn alr-hhym.*"

THE second *Lam* in *Allah*, is expressed as very short, which I before remarked under that letter in the second Chapter: and the *hha* of the last word, is prolonged by a long dash to correspond with that of *Sin* in the first.

PLATE V. No. 3.

" *Nisheslun-e-Sultaun Skander ber takht-i-padishahy bejan ec-i-padir*
" *khood.*"

" THE sitting of Prince Alexander on the royal throne, in the
" place of his father."

THIS, and the two next numbers, are specimens of the manner in which the heads of chapters are usually written; in

---

* The ninth chapter; for this omission, the Mahometan doctors account, by saying, that as this sentence bespeaks mercy, it would be misplaced at the head of a chapter denouncing vengeance. See Savary's Coran. Vol. I. p. 205.

† De particula *b* insuper notandum quod in pervulgata illa sententia, &c. &c. Wasmuth's Arab. Grammar, p. 75.

the

CHAP. V.]   PERSIAN MISCELLANIES.   75

the prefent example, the vowel-point *Damma*, giving the found of *o* or *u*, is placed over the firft letter of *Sultaun*; the diacritical points are generally blended together, and thofe of *pa* in *Padir*, expreffed by a turned figure, as mentioned in the third chapter, and given in Nos. 99, and 102, plate III. The remarks fcattered through the foregoing chapters of this work, will enable the reader to decipher without any difficulty, the words of this example; but as an additional help, I fhall give them here divefted of vowels, and exactly according to the original orthography, viz:

" *Nfhfln Sltan Skndr br tkht padfhahy bjay pdr khud.*"

FROM the *Skander Nameh*, one of the moft celebrated Romances of the Eaft, the example above given, has been extracted. This work contains the hiftory of Alexander the Great, written in admirable poetry, by *Nizàmi*, who, to a great deal of Perfian imagery and fable, has added, in this excellent poem, much curious hiftorical matter, in fome refpects, founded on, and in others, widely differing from, the Greek and Latin hiftories of the Grecian prince. Of this work, as I before mentioned, I am fortunate enough to poffefs feveral fine copies; but two particularly valuable, from a multiplicity of notes, marginal, and written between the lines in a moft minute

L 2   and

and elegant hand. Without the aid of the anonymous Perfian commentators, many paffages, I confefs, would have ftill been to me extremely difficult and obfcure; and it is hardly to be expected, that a mere European reader, without fuch affiftance, could perfectly comprehend the frequent allufions of the poet, to remote hiftory, and ancient Oriental mythology, or the variety of proper names that occur in almoft every page, both of perfons and places, and the terms ufed in fpeaking of painting, mufic, geography, &c. &c.

So very flight is the mention which M. D'Herbelôt has made of this celebrated poet*, and fo imperfect the lift which he has given of his writings, in the *Bibliotheque Orientale*, that I am induced to believe it was the purpofe of that excellent Orientalift to fpeak more fully of him, as of feveral other Perfian authors, in fome diftinct work. He flourifhed in the fixth century of the Mahometan Æra†, and the following diftich, from an elegy of *Hafiz*, (which accidentally prefents itfelf in a beautiful manufcript copy of his *Divàn*) is now, I believe, for the firft time, adduced in print, as a teftimony at once of our poet's excellence and antiquity:

نظم نظامی که چنان کهن ۱٬ نوارد جو دیج زیبا سخن

* Bibl: Orient: Articles *Nadhomi* and *Nazami*.
† The twelfth of the Chriftian Æra.

" Ze

CHAP. V.]   PERSIAN MISCELLANIES.   77

" *Ze nez'mi Nezami keh cherkh'i kohen,*
" *Nedared chu o heech zeeba'e sekhun.*"

" THE poetry of *Nezami*, in the whole circle of ancient writers, has no " equal for grace and elegance of language."

OF his works I have seen no correct list; and although I possess three copies, apparently perfect, (and one eminently beautiful) yet I am still uncertain of the exact number of his poems; one manuscript is entitled the " *Five Treasures of* " *Nezami*," and contains so many distinct compositions: in each of the other two are comprized six; but these do not correspond with the list given in Sir W. Jones's Persian Grammar (141, 3d edition.)

IN one place, already quoted, M. D'Herbélot mentions three of this author's productions, and the same number in another place; if all the works enumerated in these lists are genuine, and also those in my manuscripts, the number of Nezami's Poems would amount to nine; yet among the *Desiderata* in Eastern Literature, the late President of the Asiatic Society has mentioned a translation in prose, of " *The five Poems of Nezami**." That which I here particularly speak of, I am induced from many circumstances to regard

as

---

* See Sir John Shore's discourse, delivered, May, 1794, to the Asiatic Society, at Calcutta, the Presidency of which learned body he was called to on the death of Sir Wm. Jones, whose virtues and learning are the subject of this just and eloquent eulogium.— (European Magazine, April, 1795. Beside the poems enumerated in the list of *Nezami's* works

as an historic record of considerable authenticity; and I have not adopted this opinion merely because *Nizâmi* asserts, in the introduction to his work, that he had compiled it from the best and most ancient chronicles of the Hebrews, Greeks, and old Pahlavians*. But he skillfully rejects from his history of Alexander, many of those vain traditions, and idle fictions, which even the great *Ferdusi*, the father of Persian poetry, has admitted into his *Shah Nameh*, or " Book of Kings." Thus having mentioned some extraordinary relations concerning his hero, *Nezâmi* condemns them as " tales which wanted con-
" firmation, in the vanity of whose story there is no truth,"
—" *Guzaf-i-sekhun'ra durusty neboud,*" and acknowledging his obligations to the historians of Greece, and to the venerable Bard of *Toos* abovementioned, he regards as fabulous the prodigious circumstances which the former relate of the birth of Alexander, and rejects the tradition of *Ferdusi*, which by a strange confusion describes the Macedonian as son of Daràb the Persian king; and we find accordingly, that in the dying

---

works by Sir Wm. Jones, and Herbelòt, a short and by no means interesting composition, is ascribed to him in a printed catalogue of Persian MSS. which I have lately seen; but after a close inspection, I have reason to believe that the learned and ingenious compiler of the list, has been mistaken in assigning that trifling production to the venerable author of the *Skander Nameh*.

* See Chap. 6th of this Essay, Plate vii, No. 4.

CHAP. V.] PERSIAN MISCELLANIES. 79

scene of Darius, and his interview with Alexander, *Nezami* has suppressed the discovery that those monarchs were brothers, which in the *Shah nameh* gives an air of fable to the whole narration.

The historic poem of *Nezami*, therefore, must have escaped the ingenious *Teixeira*, who tells us that " the life and " actions of Alexander are celebrated as marvellous, by the " Persians, and described in many books, both in prose and " rhyme," &c.—yet that, " all those writers agree in asserting " that he was not the son of Philip*."

Copies of *Nezami's* work must have of late considerably multiplied, or it cannot have been that valuable history of Alexander, which, we are assured by a celebrated linguist, was so scarce, even among the Persians, about three centuries ago, that Andrew Corsaili, an intelligent foreigner, who travelled in the east, could never obtain a copy of it†.

* " La vida y hechos de Afcander Zurkharneken," (for the Arabic word *Zulkarnein*) " ò Alexandro, celebran los Parsios por maravillosos, y tienen escrito dellos muchos libros " en proza y en rima, llenos de excelentes conceptos y sentencias," &c.—" Todos los " escritores Parsios acuerdan que Afcandar no fue hijo de Philipo, a quien ellos dizen " Faylakus," &c. &c. See Relaciones y Viage dende la India, &c. &c. Oct: Amberes, 1610. Lib. I. cap. 22.

† See the " Thresor des Langues," a very curious work, by Claude Duret, (p. 498,) *Yverdun*, 1619, Quarto, where we read in his old French, that, " André Corsali en son " voyage aux Indes, asseure avoir veu entre les mains des Persans susdicts, toute l' histoire " du grand Alexandre en langue Persane de laquelle, comme de chose rare il ne sçeut onc " en retirer une copie."

But

But I reserve for a future and more convenient occasion some remarks on the *Skander Nameh*, and a few extracts and tranflations from particular and interefting paffages; and I proceed to explain the fourth fpecimen of Perfian writing, given in the mifcellaneous plate.

PLATE V. No. 4.

" *Jung kirdun-i Ruftem ba Sohràub, va kooſhtch ſhuden Sohraub az*
" *deſt-e Ruftem.*"

" THE making war (or fighting) of Ruftam with Sohraub, and
" the killing of Sohraub by the hand of Ruftam,"

IN this number I have given the title of a chapter from the celebrated *Shah Nameh*, or Book of Kings. The reader, who has perufed with attention the preceding pages of this effay, will find no difficulty in deciphering this line, of which, as written in the original, the fpelling is here given, viz.

" *Jng krdn Rſtm ba Shrab v kſhth ſhdn Shrab az dſt Rſtm.*"

I SHALL only here obferve, that in the firft word of this example *Jung* (war) the point of medial *Nun* is feparated from its letter by the intervening ftroke of *Gaf*, and that the three laſt letters of *Ruftam*, at the end of the line, are placed above the *Ra*, and the final *Ta* of the preceding word *Deſt*, the hand.

CHAP. V.]   PERSIAN MISCELLANIES.   81

THE work from which this example has been taken, is the moſt celebrated romance of the Eaſt, and has rendered immortal the name of its author, *Ferduſi* of *Toos*, who is ſtyled by orientaliſts, and well deſerves the honourable title of, " The Perſian Homer." It is a collection of the ancient traditions and Romantic ſtories of his country, containing in above ſixty thouſand couplets, a variety of heroic and amorous, hiſtorical and fabulous poems; a ſpecies of compoſition which has been always a favourite among the Perſians, after whoſe example, probably, their Arabian neighbours became lovers of romance *.

IT is certain, that above twelve centuries ago, in the days of Mohammed, the romantic ſtory of Ruſtam, which is the ſubject of the preſent example, and ſimilar tales, were popular in Perſia : returning from which country, an Arabian merchant, *Naſſer ben Hareth*, related them to his countrymen, and ſo delighted them by the narration of thoſe fictitious adventures, that they became diſguſted with the dull traditions of the Korān, and *Naſſer ben Hareth* incurred the malediction of the prophet †.

* See the admirable " Oratio de Ingenio Arabum," by the late Profeſſor H. A. Schultens, Leyden, 4to. 1788, p. 30. " —— neque tam ex ingenio Arabico fluxit, " quam ex Perſarum atque Indorum cultiore ſapientia quæ inſigniter quoque adjuvit " naturalem ingenii proclivitatem ad fictiones et fabulas Romanenſes."

† See D'Herbelôt Bibl. Orient. Art. *Naſſer ben Hareth*, &c.

M   ALLUDING

82   PERSIAN MISCELLANIES.   [CHAP. V.

ALLUDING to compofitions of this nature, an ingenious writer, who refided among the Perfians, informs us, that "they have romances of famous heroes and their deeds, among " which are pleafant rencounters, huntings, love-intrigues, " banquettings, defcriptions of flowers and delightful groves, " emphatically fet down," &c. &c *.

AND as I fhall have occafion in the courfe of this work to fpeak of the battle here mentioned, between *Ruflam* and *Sohraub*, and other romantic Perfian ftories, I difmifs the fubject for the prefent, and return to the difcuffion of manufcript difficulties.

PLATE V. No. 5.

" *Bekhaub aumedun Eufoof aleyhi àſſalàm Zeleekhara, nubet suim ve*
" *naum u mekaum oee danifteu ve b'akel u hoofh baz aumedun.*"

" The coming of Jofeph, (may peace be with him) in a dream " to Zeleekha the third time, and her learning his name and con- " dition, and her return to reafon and underftanding."

THE beautiful Zeleekha, whofe amours with the patriarch Jofeph, are celebrated by the Poet Jami, was fo diftracted by the violence of her love as to lofe all power of reafon and recol- lection, and remain deprived of her fenfes, till the appearance of the beloved youth, as above-mentioned, reftored peace to

* Dr. Fryer's Travels, p. 369, folio, 1681.

her

CHAP. V.]   PERSIAN MISCELLANIES.   83

her mind, and calmed the agitation of her foul. From a very fine copy of Jami's poem, I have extracted the lines given in this Number, being the title of a chapter, written in blue ink, and ornamented with lines of gold, &c. and in the frontifpiece is given the beginning of the fame chapter, as a fpecimen of fine poetry, written in a correct and beautiful hand.

Of this title the letters of each word, are here inferted, according to the Perfian original, viz.

"*Bkhuâb âmdu Yusf alyh alslam Zlykha'ra nubt sum,*"
"*V nam v mkam uy Danstn v bakl v bush baz amdn.*"

By the help of this mode of writing the Perfian, it will be eafy for the reader to analyze and explain to his own fatisfaction the graphical difficulties of this paffage. In the word *Yufuf*, of the firft line, he will remark that the two points of *ya* are not fituated under their proper letter, but thrown to the left under *Sin*, and that of *fa* final, in the fame word, is placed over the middle of that character.

UNDER *Alfalam* are three points, which the reader will immediately perceive to be merely ornamental, and fuperfluous, and fuch as I before mentioned in the laft page of Chapter the Third.

THE points of *ya* in *Zeleekhara*, are not placed exactly under that letter, but rather under the *Za* and *Lam*, and in the word *Nubet*, the points of final *ta* are thrown over that of the

M 2   *N*, and

84 PERSIAN MISCELLANIES. [CHAP. V.

N, and the point of *ba* placed under the ſtroke of final *ta*, which gives it the appearance of a final *ba*.

IN the ſecond line the point of *N* in *nam*, is placed to the left of the *Alif*, and under the word *Daniſten*, are three ornamental and ſuperfluous points, like thoſe above-mentioned under the word *Alſalam*; the *D* and *Alif*, are under the *N* and *S*, and the point of the initial *N* not placed over its proper letter, but to the left of it.

OF *Kaf* in *Akl*, the left point is placed over the *Lam*, the *ha* of *hooſh*, is a little turn of the pen; and in the hollow of the *Shin*, are placed the *Ba* and *Alif* of *Baz*; the *Medda* of *Aumedun*, is ſituated over the *Alif* and *Za* of *Baz*, by which circumſtance, the point of *Za* is incloſed between the two *Alifs* of *Baz* and *Aumedun*, its own letter, and the *Medda* above.

TITLES and heads of chapters, as the reader will perceive by this, and the two preceding numbers, are written in a larger character, and generally in red, blue, or golden letters, and according to the ſubject, in one, two, or more lines.

I MUST here remark, the general accuracy of the Perſians, who announce in the title of each chapter or ſection, its principal contents and ſubject. The negligence and inattention of the Arabian writers in this reſpect, are very ſerious defects, and ſtrongly reprehended by a moſt learned Orientaliſt, in a paſſage, which, as it deſcribes as well the faults of Perſian as of Arabic manuſcripts, I ſhall here inſert, in the words of the author,

" Nullus,

CHAP. V.] PERSIAN MISCELLANIES. 85

" Nullus, ut plurimum rerum index, nulla capitum fumma,
" (folemne Arabicis fcriptis vitium) occurrit, explorandis,
" enucleandifque five in experienda multiplici, ambigua, intri-
" cata fcribendi forma ; five in literis vetuftate ipfa caducis at-
" que aciem fugientibus perfpiciendis : adde vocales paffim de-
" ficientes, puncta diacritica per librariorum aut infcitiam aut
" incuriam fæpius omiffa, vel male præfixa. Adde mendofa
" vocabula, decurtatas fententias, corruptas vel dubie exaratas
" vel omnino præteritas Numerorum notas, aliaque id genus
" fcripturæ vitia que legendi atque intelligendi negotium quàm
" difficillimum effecere adeo ut vatem potius quam lectorem
" et interpretem non femel agere fim coactus*."

PLATE V. No. 6.

" *Mift to nedeedeham —— bedeedem.*"
(A fair one) " Like you I have not feen —— I have feen," &c.

IN this line, from a fonnet of the poet Sadi†, the abrupt conclufion of the fentence is marked by two little ftrokes of the pen, and a blank fpace is left between it, and the beginning of

* See the " Bibliotheca Arabico-Hifpana, of the learned *Cafiri*, preface vi. Madrid, Folio, 1760, a moft rare and valuable work, in two volumes, diftributed only in prefents by the Spanifh Court.

† For fome account of this celebrated poet and his works, See Chap. IV. p. 56, 57, &c.

another

86   PERSIAN MISCELLANIES.   [CHAP. V.

another fentence, in which the lover declares that he had feen the lovelieft fair one's of the earth, but none equal to the miftrefs whom he addreffes.

PLATE V. No. 7.

" *Maunend too audmy der afak*
" *Memkin neboud——peri nedeedem.*"
" No human creature in this world
" Was ever equal to you——I have not feen a fairy."

THIS diftich is, likewife, from the poet *Sàdi*, and I give it as a rare inftance of the conclufion of a fentence afcertained by a blank fpace left between it and that which follows. Its graphical difficulties are fo few, that the lines written *ad literam*, will explain them.

" *Mannd tu admy dr afak*
" *Mmkn nbud——pry ndydm.*"

THE extraordinary degree of beauty which the Perfians affign to the imaginary being called *Peri*, may be conceived from the extravagant compliment paid by the poet to his miftrefs, in the firft fentence of this diftich. Of the Peries I fhall fpeak

CHAP. V.] PERSIAN MISCELLANIES. 87

speak more fully in the next chapter, and I shall in this place only observe, that so excessive in their admiration of beauty are the amorous Persians, that those who possess it in an eminent degree, are considered by them as something more than mortal. Of this opinion is the celebrated poet *Khosrù*, in the beginning of one of his sonnets, from the Divan, or collection of his poems.

" *Khoobaun gumaun meber keh az awlad-i Admy' end*
" *Hour' end ya serishteh va ya ruah azem' end.*

" Think not that beautiful damsels are of the human race:
" They are houries of Paradise, or angels, or superior spirits."

PLATE V. No. 8.

In this number are given the Persian numerical figures, as I have found them described in several well-written books. I have before remarked (page 70.) that when the word *Seh*, *three*, is expressed by letters, the numerical character is generally placed over the stroke of *Sin*. It is to be observed, that the Persian numerical figures are to be read, as with us, from left to right.

In the lower lines of this example are given, in Persian figures, the dates of the last year, according to the Mahometan
and

and Chriſtian Æras; or, as the latter is ſtyled in Aſia, " the " year of the Meſſiah *."

PLATE V. No. 9.

" *Neby ſad deſteh-e-reihaun peiſh bulbul*
" *Nekhahed khatereſh juz nekhet-a-gul.*"

" You may place an hundred handfuls of fragrant herbs and flowers before
" the nightingale;
" Yet he wiſhes not, in his conſtant heart, for more than the ſweet breath
" of his beloved roſe."

IN this couplet from the poet Jamì I have given an example of the fanciful manner in which the Perſians often write

---

* An index of the correſponding years is prefixed to the ſecond volume of Richardſon's Arab. and Perſ. Dictionary, calculated to the year 1900 of our æra, of the Hegira, 1318.

The learned Profeſſor Tychſen has given ſome rules for thoſe who wiſh to aſcertain the year of the Hegira, correſponding with any particular year of the Chriſtian æra. See his " Introductio in Rem Numariam Muhammedanorum," 8vo. Roſtoch, 1794. p. 36.

I have before quoted this author, (p. 3.) whoſe knowledge of the Eaſtern languages is extenſive; and his peculiar ſkill in deciphering the moſt ancient and difficult Arabic inſcriptions, carved in the Cufic character, ſo ingenuouſly and honourably acknowledged by his learned antagoniſt, the Italian Abbè *Aſſimani*, Profeſſor of Oriental Languages at Padua, in his letter of November, 1788, wherein he ſays, " Vi ſiete un portento nel " decifrare cio che ad altri ſembra indicifrabile. Vi ſiete talmente addimeſticato colla " ſcrittura Cufica che non vè alcuno che poſſa uguagliarvi." See p. 32. Appendix Interpr. Inſcr. Cuf. among the Quatuor Opuſcula, &c. of Tychſen, before quoted, p. 3, Roſtoch, 4to. 1794.

ſome

CHAP. V.]   PERSIAN MISCELLANIES.   89

fome ftriking paffages, particularly in pages oppofite to a miniature painting, or other embellifhments. As this fpecimen requires fome explanation, I fhall endeavour to point out and remove its principal difficulties, by a minute analyfis of every word, and enable the reader to afcertain the exact number and arrangement of the letters, by the following lines, in which the original fpelling is adhered to.

" Nhy fd dfth ryhhn pyfh blbl,
" Nkhuahd khatrfh jz nkht gl."

IN the firft word *Neby*, the point of *N*, is not placed over its proper letter, and the final *ya* is without points; the *Dal* of *Sad* is little more than the termination of the thick ftroke, connecting it with the preceding letter. See under *Dal*, in the fecond Chapter.

IN *Dofteh*, the *d* is placed under the ftroke of *Sin*, and the final *ha* expreffed by a thick rounded turn of the pen, over which nearly, is placed the letter *Ra*, beginning the next word *Reihaun*, where the reader will obferve, that a long ftroke ferves for the body of *ya*, that its points alone diftinguifh it, and that thefe are rather placed under the *hha*. The *Alif* is a mere hair-ftroke, and over the final *Nun*, are placed the two firft letters of *Peifh*; and the points of *Shin* in that word. Thofe of *pa* and *ya*, are thrown together under the ftroke of *Shin*, and in

N   the

the curve of *Shin*, is placed the point of the initial *Ba* of *Bulbul*. The medial *Ba* of *Bulbul*, has its point clofe below it; but that of the initial *Ba* is placed in the hook of *Shin*, belonging to the preceding word.

THE fecond line begins with *Khahed*, the negative particle *N* being prefixed, and for this particle, we find nothing more than a long hair-ftroke, marked however by the diacritical point of *Nun*. That of *Kha*, is placed to the left of its proper letter, the *Alif* is a fimple hair-ftroke, the *ha* is a little reverfed comma, joined to the final *Dal* by a turn of the pen. The point of *Kha* in *Khatr*, touches the top of *Alif*. The *Ra* is abruptly joined to the *Ta*, and the points of final *Shin*, are thrown over the firft indenture of that letter.

THE point of *Jim* in *Juz*, is placed in the hook of the preceding *Shin* of *Khaterfh*, and the point of *Za* low down, and to the left fide of the letter.

IN the word *Nekhet*, the point of *Nun*, is not exactly over its letter, and the body of *Caf*, is expreffed by a longer ftroke than is ufual, the upper or oblique ftroke is a little inflected, and the lower part of the letter joined to the fucceeding *ha* in a very fudden and abrupt manner. The *ha* runs into the final *ta*, by a turn of the pen.

THE *Gaf* of the word *Gul*, is defcribed as a fmall circle, adhering to the perpendicular ftroke of *Lam*, with its oblique ftroke proceeding from it.

THE

CHAP. V.] PERSIAN MISCELLANIES. 91

THE exceffive delight which the Perfian nightingale derives from the enjoyment of the rofe's fragrance, affords a thoufand beautiful allufions and allegories to the eaftern poets: In a line from one of the fonnets by the celebrated Sàdi, he pays to his miftrefs the moft delicate compliment that a Perfian lover could exprefs, by faying,

" *Bulbul ar rzoee tzo beened tulb-e- Gul nekund**."

" Should the nightingale once behold thy beauteous face, he would no
" longer feek his beloved rofe."

To account for this allegorical paffion entertained by the nightingale for the rofe, and which is the fubject of fo much beautiful imagery in Perfian poetry, we muft confider that the plaintive voice of that fweet bird, is firft heard at the fame feafon of the year in which the rofe begins to blow; by a natural affociation of ideas, they are therefore connected as the conftant and infeparable attendants of the fpring. It is probable too, that the nightingale's favourite retreat may be the rofe garden, and the leaves of that flower occafionally his food: but it is certain that he is delighted with its fmell, and

---

* The word in this line which I have here written *ar*, according to the Perfian orthography, is a contraction of *agur* if; moftly ufed in poetry.

sometimes indulges in the fragrant luxury (if I may be allowed the expreſſion) to ſuch exceſs, as to fall from the branch, intoxicated and helpleſs, to the ground*.

PLATE VI. No. 1.

—" *Chunauncheh herdoo ajz keſhtend—Nuzim—*
" *Bedil goſt Ruſtam keh imrooze jaun,*"
" *Bemauned bemen zendeham jawedaun"—*
" *Hemidoon bedil goſt Deev-i-ſepeed,*
" *Keh az jaun-è ſhireen ſhudem na'aumeed."—*.

" *Chun her doo as guſhty giriftun hail ſhudend ſâaty derung*
" *Nemudend; Ruſtam deed keh az khoon-a-Dive rooe-e-zemeen gùl*
" *ſhud.*

IN theſe lines I have given the words, (though not arranged in the ſame order as thoſe in the engraved ſpecimen) of a paſſage from a Perſian manuſcript, deſcribing the ſingle combat of the celebrated *Ruſtam*, with his very formidable antagoniſt, the *Dive,* or *Dew-Sepeed;* they fought with unre-

---

* See Jones's Remarks on this ſubjeƈt and a beautiful paſſage from the *Shah Nameh* of Ferduſi, in his Latin Commentaries on Aſiatic poetry, p. 140, &c.
See alſo the *Religio Veterum Perſarum* of the moſt learned Hyde, p. 342. (Oxf. 1700) " Cæterum in Oriente Luſciniæ Roſas odorari ſolent, â roſa ad roſam volando et " odorando, donec planè inebrientur et cadant, ita ut a quovis capiantur," &c. &c.

mitting

.N°7.

چنانچہ ہر دو عاجز گشتہ نظام بلبل گفت رستم کہ اے دژ زنجان یا بہانہ
ممکن زندہ برجا دان؟؟ امیدوان بدل گفت دیو سپہ؟ که از زنجان
ترس نشدم نا امید؛؟ چون ہر دو از کشتی گرفتن
مائل شدند ساعتی درنگ نمودند رستم دید کہ از خون
دیو روی زمین گل شد

.N°8.

جیحون پنج نام
رود یست در بلخ و در حدیث آمدہ است کہ چہار جوی از
بہشت فرود آمدہ اند جیحون و سیحون و دجلہ و فرات کہ در کودا

.N°9.

پارہ از شب گذشت
برای رستم فرش خواب کردہ اسپنہ رستم در خواب شد بعد از ساعتی
دید کہ نازنین ماہ پیکر اتو پیش پر دہ پشت کنیزی درپیش او
شمع بدست گرفتہ آمد و رمش رستم نشست نظم زیر روی بر آمدگی
ماہ روی؟؟ چو چو خورشید تابان پر از رنگ و بوی؟؟

CHAP. V.] PERSIAN MISCELLANIES. 93

mitting fury for a confiderable time,—" So that" to ufe the words of the fpecimen: "—They both became weary and faint." " Poetry—" In his heart (to himfelf) faid Ruftam, Oh that this " day my life, may remain with me, and I fhall furely live for " ever!"—At the fame time the *Dive-Sepeed* faid within himfelf, " Alas! I have no hope of faving my precious life."— " When after a long and dreadful ftruggle they paufed for a " while, Ruftam perceived, that from the blood of his adver- " fary, the earth was ftained with purple, or that the face of " the earth had affumed the colour of rofes."

TO render the deciphering of the original as eafy as poffible to the beginner, I fhall here give the Perfian words, placed exactly in the order of the engraved fpecimen, and as in that divefted of their vowels:

1. " Chnanch hr du ajz kfhtnd—NZM—bdl gft Rftm kh amruz jan :: bmanJ
2. " bmn zndham javdan :: hmydun bdl gft dyv fpyd :: kh az jan
3. " fhyryn fhdm naamyd :: chun hr du az gfhty grftn
4. " hayl fhdnd faaty drnk nmudnd Rftm dyd kh az khun
5. " dyv ruy zmyn gl fhd."

The writing of this fpecimen, although fufficiently accurate, is far from being elegant: the points of the two *Chims* in the

the firſt word are confuſed, as are thoſe of *Pa* and *Ya*, in *Sepeed*, (ſecond line.) The reader will perceive, that throughout the whole example, final *Ya* is deſtitute of points. In the word *Kuſtam*, which occurs both in the firſt and fourth lines, the indented ſtroke of *Sin* is brought above the *Ra*. In the laſt word *(Bemaned)* of the firſt line, as in the firſt word *(Bemen)* of the ſecond, the initial *Ba* is to be known by little more than its point. In the third line, the letters *Shin*, *Ya*, and *Ra*, of *Shireen*, are run abruptly one into another; and the laſt word of that line, the *Ra*, proceeds in almoſt a ſtraight line from the lower part of *Gaf*.

THIS, and the two other examples given in the ſame plate, are from manuſcripts written in the coarſe and haſty manner of the Indian Munſhees: the reader muſt not expect, therefore, in ſuch writings, to have his eye delighted with graceful flouriſhes, minute hair-ſtrokes, or elegant combinations.

AMONG the moſt celebrated romances of the Eaſt, whether founded on hiſtory or fable, the *Shâh-nameh*, or Book of Kings, which unites both, is juſtly eſteemed the firſt: and has gained the ſame degree of fame to its immortal author, *Ferdooſi* (or *Firdauſi*) among the Perſians, as the compoſition of the Odyſſey and Iliad, has done for Homer among the Greeks.

CHAP. V.] PERSIAN MISCELLANIES. 95

Greeks*. Like thefe, the Perfian poem defcribes kings and heroes, protected or perfecuted by fuperhuman powers : relates the adventures of perfonages who never exifted but in the poet's imagination : and of others whofe exiftence is dubious, though not improbable. The *Shah Nameh*, however, defcends to the ages of kings and heroes, whom authentic hiftory acknowledges.

But in the prefent fpecimen, the poet defcribes the dreadful combat of the famous *Ruflam*, who may be ftyled the Perfian Hercules, with an imaginary being endued with preternatural qualities; which, in fome refpects, may be found to correfpond with the Demigods of Greece, though not in all; and particularly in the effential qualification of immortality.

For, although the *Dives* are fuppofed to live very long, yet, like the gentle *Peries*, another creature of Perfian imagination, their lives are limited; and, from the defcriptions of their battles, we find that they were obnoxious to the blows of an human foe. From the malignancy of their nature, the Dives waged war not only with mankind, but perfecuted with unremitting ferocity the Peries, a race of beings to which they were as oppofite as imagination can conceive; differing in all refpects, fex, difpofition, and appearance: the Peries being

* For anecdotes of Ferdufi, See the " Anthologia Perfica," p. 80, &c. 4to. Vienna, 1778; and, " Champion's Poetical Tranflation of Part of the *Shah Nameh*," 4to. 1791.

female,

female, gentle, amiable, and beautiful: their enemies, the Dives, all males, cruel, wicked, and of the moſt hideous aſpect *.

But I find that the idea of *Dive*, or *Dew*, is very vague, even among the Perſians, as indeed muſt ever be the caſe where poetic fancy can add properties and attributes at will. In a manuſcript before me, which mentions the *Ghùl* (or ſpecies of dæmon, ſuppoſed to dwell in deſarts, or church-yards, and to devour men and beaſts) under that word ſome Perſian annotator has written *Dive*, as ſynonymous, or rather, as the word in Perſian approaching neareſt to the ſenſe of the former, which is Arabic.

And the poet Nizàmi, in the beginning of his *Skander Nameh*, implores the divine protection againſt the *Dive*, or *Dew*; as it were the great *Dive*, which a marginal note explains by *Shëetaun*, Satan, or the Devil. This word is Arabic, from the Hebrew שטן the proper Perſian name being *Aherimàn*, for which the word *Dive* is now generally uſed †.

* The idea which the Aſiatics entertain of thoſe imaginary beings, is very plainly expreſſed in the following deſcription of their painted repreſentations. "At Lahor in "the Mogul's Palace, pictures of Dews or Dives, intermixt in moſt ugly ſhapes, with "long hornes, ſlaringe eyes, ſhagge hair, great fangs, ugly pawes, long tailes, with "ſuch horrible difformity and deformity, that I wonder the poore women are not "frightened therewith."—See William Finch's Obſervations, &c. in Purchas's Pilgrims, Vol. I. 433. in 5 vols. folio. 1625.

† " Pessimum humani Generis hoſtis—apud modemiores is vocatur Div." &c. Hyde's " Relig. Vet. Perſ. 162."

CHAP. V.] PERSIAN MISCELLANIES.

THE manuscript from which I have extracted the specimen in question, is an abridgement of the great *Shah Nameh*, by Ferdusi; a work written entirely in verse, but here abridged in prose, with passages of the original poetry occasionally interspersed.

THE combatants *Rustam*, and the *Dive Sepeed*, or White Dive, had fought for a considerable time, with nearly equal success; for we read in this passage, that weary and exhausted they suspended their blows, and each within himself despaired of escaping from his adversary's sword: "If he could survive "that day, the Persian warrior would consider himself as im- "mortal,"—and the Demon despaired of saving his "sweet "life*". Of this, the hero *Rustam*, soon deprived him, for seeing the ground stained by the blood that gushed in torrents from the monster's wounds, he rushed on him with confidence and renewed vigour, flung him to the earth, and tore his malignant heart from the mutilated and hideous corse: this combat is the subject of a painting, which lately ornamented the entrance into a public building at Shirauz†.

---

* A Grecian hero, in nearly the same predicament, uses a similar expression: the *Janu Shireen* of *Ferdusi*, is the φιλον ητορ of Homer, in the speech of Hector, who had almost expired, in consequence of a wound received from Ajax. Iliad, B. 15, 251.

† "At the door of the Ark, is a painting done in very lively colours, representing the "combat between the celebrated Persian hero *Rustam* and *Deeb Sifeed* or the *White Dæmon*. "The story is taken from Ferdusi's Shah Nama, and the figures are at full length, but "ill proportioned." Francklin's Tour from Bengal to Persia, p. 55. Lond. 8vo. 1790.

OF the many romantic stories concerning Ruſtam, it is highly probable that some historic facts have been the foundation, though the authentic records of them cannot now be found, or if they still exist, must remain unexplained, till a key be discovered to the Persepolitan inscriptions. His fame, as an extraordinary hero, was celebrated in the Romances of Persia, (as I before mentioned, p. 81,) above twelve centuries ago; he is supposed by some, to have been contemporary with Artaxerxes, or Ahazuerus; his tomb is still shewn to travellers, and tradition has affixed his name to a gigantic figure cut in stone, near the ruins of ancient Persepolis, now called *Chehelminâr*, or the "Forty Pillars."—And near the city of Shirauz, is an immense quadrangular monument, in commemoration of Ruſtam's victorious combat with the Deev Sepeed, or White Demon*.

---

* This is the *Kelaât-i Deev Sepeed*, or Caſtle of the White Giant, which Father Angelo, in his Gazophylacium Persicum, p. 127, declares to have been the moſt venerable monument of antiquity, which he had ſeen in Perſia, " *Antiquita la più auguſta ch' habbi* " *io veduto in Perſia:*" built, according to tradition, on the ſpot where the Demon fell, by whom, probably, is typified ſome cruel and powerful tyrant, whom Ruſtam oppoſed and conquered. Gazoph: Perſic: Folio, Amſterd. 1684.

PLATE

CHAP. V.] PERSIAN MISCELLANIES. 99

PLATE VI. No. 2.

" *Jaihoon lefatha nam'e rudi eſt der Balkh, wa der hedyz aumedebeſt* " *keh chehar jawy az behiſht frud aumede'nd, Jaihon, va Shaihoon, va* " *Dejleh, va Forât, keh der Cufeh eſt.*"

" JAIHOON, with the orthographical mark Fatha, is the name of " a river in Balkh: (Tranſoxania or Choraſſan) and it is tra- " ditionally ſaid that four ſtreams deſcend from Paradiſe: the " Jaihoon, the Shaihoon, the Dejleh, and the Euphrates, which is " in Cuſa, or Chaldea."

THIS ſpecimen is given from a Ferhung, or Perſian Dictionary, (article *Jaihoon*) and will ſerve to ſhew how proper names are diſtinguiſhed in ſuch works. Over the word *Jaihoon, Shaihoon, Dejleh,* and *Forât,* are placed thoſe marks of diſtinction, already mentioned in the explanation of Plate V. No. 10.— A mark of the ſame kind is alſo placed over the beginning of one ſentence, and after the end of another in the ſecond line.— The words in the original order and orthography, are thus:

1. " *Jyhhun lfthh nam*
2. " *Rudyſt dr Blk u dr hhdys amdh aſt kh chhar Juy az*
3. " *Bhſht frud amdand Jyhun u Shyhhun u Djlh u Frat kh dr Kuſhoſt.*"

O 2   IN

IN the firſt word of this example, the reader will obſerve, that the body of *bha*, comes between the letter *ya*, and its diacritical points: in the word *Befutha*, the points of *ta* are rather placed over the final *bha*. In the ſecond line the *ya of rudy eſt* has not its points placed exactly under it; and the point of *Ba* in *Balkh*, is within the hollow of final *Kha*; the points of *bha* in *hedys* are not exactly under that letter, and the *Alif* of *Aſt* is below the *Sin* and *Ta*. The point of *Chim*, in *Chebar*, (for three points) is placed very low, and the *ha* expreſſed by a kind of upright comma; the point of *Jim* in *Juwy*, ſeems rather to belong to the *Vaw*. In the third line, the laſt ſyllable of *Amedand*, is placed at a diſtance from the former part of the word; the final *Nun* of *Shihoon*, has its point thrown above it; the final *ha* in *Dejleh*, as in the word *Keh*, both in the ſecond and third line, is expreſſed by a ſhort turn of the pen, alſo in *Cufeh*; the laſt word *Aſt* is divided, and the *Sin* and *Ta* thrown above the line. In Perſian Lexicons, the article or word to be looked for is written in red ink.

IN this ſpecimen of Perſian definition, we find the names of four very celebrated rivers, of which the *Jaihoon*, or *Gihon*, (the *Oxus*,) is the firſt in order. It riſes in the Province of Sogdiana,

diana, among the mountains of Imaus, which feparate *Iraun,* or Perfia, from *Turaùn,* the country of the ancient Scythians. This River is alfo called *Amù,* by the Afiatics, and *Bactros,* by the Greek and Roman writers, probably from *Bokhara,* a city and province which it bounds[*].

THE waters of this famous River fall into the Cafpian or Hircanian Sea, which, from the bordering countries, has been called by the Perfians, " The Sea of Khoraffan, or of Gilaùn— *Deriya-i-Gilauni.*"

AMONG his other titles, the Perfian Emperor ftyled himfelf " Lord of the four Rivers of Paradife, which an ingenious traveller, (Sir Thomas Herbert, p. 225,) explains by " Euphrates, Tigris, Araxes, and Indus ;" although in another place, (p. 243,) he acknowledges his uncertainty, whether thefe were the ftreams that watered that happy garden; that the Euphrates and Tigris, were the principal rivers of the terreftrial Paradife, is allowed by all writers. The *Jihoon,* or *Oxus,* as we have juft feen, is fuppofed by fome to have its fource there, but as to the river *Shihoon,* as written in the

---

[*] The moft accurate and ingenious Geographer of the prefent day, is not, however, of opinion that the modern *Bokhara* is the Bactria of the Ancients : That it is fuppofed fo, he confiders, like many other prevailing notions, as a geographical mifconception.— See Rennel's Memoir of a Map of Hindooftan. P. 199. Second Edition. Quarto, London. 1792.

fpecimen,

specimen, I muſt confeſs my ignorance. I cannot affirm that it means the *Araxes*, which riſes in Armenia, to the Weſt of the Caſpian Sea; and I ſhould rather imagine that the points over the firſt letter were ſuperfluous, and that it ſignifies the *Sihoon*, or ancient *Jaxartes*, between which, and the lower part of the courſes of the *Jihoon*, or *Oxus*, lies that country called Tranſoxania formerly, and by the modern Aſiatics, *Mawer'-ul Neher*, "The Land beyond the River."

But ſo little has been done on the geography of thoſe countries, and ſo ignorant are we ſtill of the exact ſituation of the rivers which we ſpeak of, that a moſt learned writer takes particular occaſion to remark the peculiar obſcurity which yet hangs about them*; and even the celebrated Orientaliſt, M. D. Herbelôt, only tells us, that perhaps *("peut-être")* the *Shihoon*, " is only another name for that river, which the " Ancients called *Jaxartes*, and the Arabs write *Sihoon*†."

Of the river Tigris, ſo celebrated by the Greek and Latin writers, the ancient name is no longer uſed, and it is now called

---

* " De Araxe—Magnam et hic fluvius Geographiæ obſcuritatem adtulit, dum diverſis adeò locis deſcribitur, &c."

" De Oxu et Jaxarte; Nuſquam major eſt Geographiæ obſcuritas et ignorantia quam in tractu qui mare ſive lacum et regnum Sinenſe interjacet."—See p. 541, and 544, of Is. Voſſius's Notes on Pomponius Mela. 8vo. Leyden. 1722.

† Biblioth. Orient. Art. " Scheikhoan;" " C'eſt peut-être le nom de la même Riviere que les Arabes appellent autrement Sihon, &c."

Dejleh;

CHAP. V.] PERSIAN MISCELLANIES. 103

Dejleh; the etymology of the former is traced to the Perfian word *Teer* an arrow, which the river, from its velocity, was faid to refemble*. To this word the Greeks (according to their ufual cuftom of adapting to their own idiom, all foreign, or as they ftyle them *barbarous*, words) added the common termination of the nominative cafe *is*, and the interpolation of the Greek *gamma* may be accounted for by the probable gutturality of pronunciation with which the Perfians uttered the letter *R*.†

THE rapidity of this river's courfe is alluded to by Sadi, in an elegy which has been publifhed with a Latin tranflation. " The fame of my verfes," fays the prophetic poet, " fhall " fpread over the world with greater impetuofity than the current of the Tigris‡;" and the river Dejleh is celebrated in a particular chapter of a moft excellent Geographical poem by *Khacani*.§

* " Tigris a celeritate quâ defluit, Tigri nomen inditum eft quia Perfica lingua Tigrim sagittam appellant. Quint. Curt.—See the various notes of Pupma, Cellarius, Loccenius, and other learned critics in Snakenberg's moft excellent edition of Quint. Curtius. 4to, 1724, lib. 4, cap. 9, 255.

† A guttural pronunciation of feveral letters, fcarcely to be attained by foreigners, is a ftriking charaéteriftic of all the Eaftern languages; the letter *ghain*, in particular, approaches in fome inftances to the roughnefs of a croaking *R.*—See Richardfon's Arab. and Perf. Dict. Vol. II. p. 6.

‡ The original is given in the Anthologia Perfica, p. 50, 4to. Vienna, 1788.

§ The " *Tohfet al Irakein*," a fine defcription in Verfe of the two *Iraks*, Arabian and Perfian Provinces,—See particularly the chapter intituled " *Der Suffet-i-Dejleh hezeret'e Bagdad.*"

4   THE

THE ancient Medes as well as Persians (according to Pliny) called an arrow *Tigris*, and a learned commentator on Plutarch contends that this is properly a *Medic*, not a *Persian* word*; but the two nations are confounded by most authors, on account of their vicinity. Yet, though all ancient writers agree, that the name, whether *Medic* or *Persian*, was imposed as expressive of the rapidity of this river's current, we find one traveller who calls them all in question, and asserts, that its stream is less swift, even than that of the Euphrates†.

" ON the banks of the *Dejleh*, " am I fallen," (says the plaintive poet *Jami*) " unfriended, and remote from any habi-
" tation, whilst a torrent of tears, like that of the rapid stream,
" flows from my eyes‡." This river, from its conflux with the Euphrates, may be said to water the plains of Babylon, and I could never read the above-mentioned passage, in the original

---

* " Plin. VI. 27, and Maussacus in Not: ad Plut. de Flum.
† " Pietro della Valle, Epist. 17.
‡ The poet Jami, dwells with much feeling on his sufferings in this place, for he repeats, in nearly the same words, the passage above given, in two poems of his Divaûn, and, I believe in others,—

" *Ber kunar-i Dejleh am auftadeh, dur az khan u maun,*
" *Wa az doo deedeh Dejleh-i khoon der kunar men ruvàn.*"

And one of his *Gazels*, or Sonnets, thus begins:

" *Ber kunar-i Dejleh dur az yar va mehjur az dyar,*
" *Darem az afhk-i chekur gosu Dejleh-i khoon der kunar.*" .

CHAP. V.]   PERSIAN MISCELLANIES.   105

Persian, without recollecting the beautiful beginning of that fine Hebrew psalm or elegy, composed in a similar forlorn situation, and expressive of the same feelings*.

FROM the original Chaldaic name פרת The Greeks have formed their corrupt Ευφρατης; for it is vain to seek the etymology of this word in a Greek compound.† The Persians and Arabians still call the river by its ancient Hebrew name, which they write, as in the engraved specimen *Fràt*.

THE celebrated current of the Euphrates, was divided, according to the Arabian geographer, whom *Bochart* follows‡, into five channels or branches, one of which led to *Cufa* in Chaldea; and on the banks of another, was seated the

---

* " By the waters of Babylon we sat down and wept, &c. &c.——Psalm cxxxvii.

The beginning of Goldsmith's " Traveller" will also recur to one's mind, on reading the Persian passage :

" Remote, unfriended, melancholy, slow,
" Or by the lazy Scheld, or wandering Po," &c.

† Thus Pliny would derive it from Ευφραινω, *latificare*, because, in its stagnations, this river fertilized the soil, and thereby delighted the inhabitants of the adjacent plains. Derivations of this kind, are spoken of thus by the learned Selden—(*Diis Syris, Astoreth)* " Multo magis enim nugantur Græculi."—" Sua in lingua origines hujusmodi ridicule quærentes"—and by another learned Orientalist, Relandus, (in his " Dissert. de ver. ling. " Pers: article Paradise"—)" Ridiculi sunt Græci qui Paradisi etymon ex suo " sermone ducunt"—Yet Pliny's derivation seems borrowed from the more direct radix " of the Hebrew name פרה fructum ferre, &c.

‡ Geographia Sacra Phaleg. 38.—Cadomi, folio, 1646.

P   " Golden

"*Golden Babylon*"* once the proud miftrefs of the eaftern world, being the capital of the Affyrian monarchy, which comprehended Syria, Mefopotamia, Chaldea, Perfia; in fhort, except India, all the great nations of weftern Afia.

On the banks of thofe celebrated ftreams, the נהרות בבל *Neheroth Babel*, or " Rivers of Babylon," of the royal Pfalmift, the perfecuted Jews hung up their ufelefs harps, nor would gratify " thofe who had led them captive into the " ftrange land with melody, or with a fong†." Thofe banks were fo thickly planted with willow trees, as the learned Bochart informs us, that the country of Babylon was thence ftyled " The Vale of Willows‡," and on thofe trees were fufpended the neglected and unftrung lyres of the captive Hebrews.

At Babylon, probably, the ancient Perfians learned the arts of magic incantation from the conquered Chaldeans§. The witchcraft of Babel is mentioned in the Korân, and alluded to by numberlefs Arabian and Perfian writers; and to the Epoch of the Babylonian conqueft, we may trace the multitude of Chaldaic words, that are to be found in the *Pahlavì*, or ancient language of Perfia.

In the arrangement and names of the Rivers, as given in the engraved Specimen, we find a confiderable deviation from

* " Βαβυλων πολυχρυσος,"—Æfchyl. Perfæ.   † Pfalm cxxxvii.
‡ Geogr. Sacr. Phaleg. 40.   § See Potter's note to Æfchylus's Perfians."

CHAP. V.]   PERSIAN MISCELLANIES.   107

the Mosaic account of Paradise, or at least, the Hebrew names must have lost their original signification, or, as is generally supposed, the Septuagint have been mistaken, in making *Pison*, to be the River *Ganges*, and *Gihon*, the *Nile*. But indeed, so vague is the knowledge we have of the terrestrial Paradise, that although most writers agree, in supposing its situation to have been at the conflux of the Tigris and Euphrates, yet some have supposed it placed in Arabia Felix (as St. Augustine,) others near the North Pole, in Egypt, &c. &c. The four rivers mentioned by Moses, which descended from it, were the *Pison*, the *Gihon*, the *Hiddekel*, and the *Euphrates*; yet the learned Milton was conscious of the uncertainty attending a particular description of those rivers, and the countries through which they flow, when, in the fourth book of his " Paradise Lost," he wisely contents himself with mention of the four streams, " whereof needs no account."

THAT the Nile was one of those rivers, seems to have been formerly a popular notion. I shall quote here a passage from an ancient Pilgrim's Journal, who travelled in the Holy Land, about the year 1400, the original manuscript of which is preserved in the Cottonian Library.

" In Egipt is a Citie faire
" That hight Massar or else Karo,*

* *Cairo*, or *Mesr*, the capital of Egypt, of which the Arabic name, (from the Hebrew) is still *Mesr*.

P 2   " In

" In the which mony chirches bee,
" And oon is of our Lady—
" De Columpna calleth hit is
" And fent Barbara beriet there is
" There is a water of gret prife
" That cometh out of Paradife,
" The which is calleth Nilus
" Men of that land thei faie thuse
" Alfo there is a gret Gardeyn
" Where that the Bawm groeth in," &c.*

THAT four rivers had their fources in Paradife or Eden has alfo been a Rabbinical opinion: but they are defcribed as very different from any of the rivers before mentioned— " thence" (fays a Jewifh author, fpeaking of Paradife) " flow four ftreams, to wit, of milk, of wine, of balfam, and of honey."† The rivers defcribed by Mofes, a celebrated Orientalift believes to be the Phafis, Araxes, Tigris, and Euphrates, among whofe fources in Armenia, he fuppofes the earthly paradife to have been fituated‡; according to Milton it was placed on the banks of the Tigris; and his learned

* See " Purchas's Pilgrims," vol. ii. p. 1243, folio, 5 Vols, 1625.
† The words of this Rabinical writer are, in the original Hebrew,

ומושכין ממנה ד׳ נהרות אחד של הלב אחד של יין אחד של אפרסמון אחד של דבש

See Dav; Millii Differt. de Mahamedifmo ante Mohamedem. p. 89. 4to, Leyden, 1743.
‡ Relandi Differt. de Situ Paradifi Terreftris, p. 4.

commentator

CHAP. V.]   PERSIAN MISCELLANIES.   109

commentator (Newton) is of opinion that the united currents of that river, and the Euphrates, in the words of the poet,

> " Now divided into four main ſtreams,
> " Run diverſe, watering many a famous realm," &c.
> " Rolling on orient pearls and ſands of gold."—
>   Par. Loſt, B. 4, 233.

But as a farther purſuit of antiquities would ſeduce me from my original plan, and encroach on the ſubject of a future publication : for accounts of Egypt, Aſſyria, and Perſia, I refer the reader to thoſe authors, who have treated of their ancient hiſtory : to Herodotus particularly for the deſcription of Old Babylon's extent and ſplendour; and to the learned Preſident of the Aſiatic Society, for Remarks on the Chaldaic Words, found in the Sanſcrit and Perſian languages*.

And I ſhall cloſe my obſervations on this ſpecimen, by remarking the extreme reſpect and veneration in which great rivers have been held by all nations†. The Nile, whoſe

---

* See " Sir Wm. Jones's Anniverſary Diſcourſe, 1789."—Aſiatic Reſearches.

† The ancient Perſians regarded all rivers with extreme veneration, as we learn from Herodotus: (Clio) and the reſpect which they, after the ancient Cuthites, paid to fountains and ſtreams in general, became prevalent alſo among other nations, ſo as at one time, to be almoſt univerſal.—See Bryant's Analyſis of Ancient Mythology, and Beloe's Notes on Herodotus.

ſubſiding

subsiding waters left fertility on the burning soil of Egypt, was the most important object of public observation, and mystically represented by various Hieroglyphics; and to the Ganges divine honours are paid, and the Indian is happy, who can expire on its sacred banks. Our ancient classics always traced any celebrated current, to the copious urn of some river Deity; but the Mahometans, adopting the old traditions of Chaldea, which placed Terrestrial Paradise on the banks of the confluent Tigris and Euphrates, and from a religious abhorrence of Polytheism, not being at liberty to derive their favourite streams from any subordinate Divinity, have assigned to them at once a Paradisaical source, and placed their fountains in the Garden of Eden.

PLATE VI. No. 3.

———" *Paureh az sheb guzesht : beray Rùstam serish-i khaùb* " *kesteraneed : Rùstam der khaùb shùd; baad az sàaty deed keh Nazu-* " *neen mahe peiker az pes'a perdeh pidaw shud : Keneezy der peish o* " *shumaà bedost giristeh aumed, wa der peish Rùstam nesheft : NUSIM-* " *ze perdeh ber aumed yeky Mah-a rooce,"—" Chu khorsheed tabaun por* " *as rung u buee."*

" Part of the night thus passed away; a splendid couch was
" spread with cushions for Rùstam, on which he laid himself down to
" rest; after a short while, he beheld a beauteous damsel, lovely as the
" moon,

CHAP. V.]   PERSIAN MISCELLANIES.   111

" moon, who advanced from behind the tapeftry, holding a lighted
" taper in her hand, and placed herfelf near him:"—POETRY. "From
" the hangings, advanced a moon-faced damfel, bright as the Sun,
" with glowing complexion, and fweet perfumes."

IN this fpecimen, as in the firft number of the fame plate, the reader will remark, that the word *Nuzim*, (written always in red ink) denotes that a paffage in verfe immediately follows, confifting of more than one couplet; the word *Beit*, is ufed when the verfe is of one diftich only; in the prefent example, although I have given but one couplet, yet the word *Nuzim*, is applied, becaufe in the original, feveral lines of poetry follow: for the little figures inclofing verfes, fee Plate, No. V. 1.

OF this fpecimen, the principal graphical difficulties will be explained by the following lines, written in the order of the original:

Line 1 " Parh az fhb gzfht
2 " Bray rftm frfh khuab kftranyd rftm dr khuab fhd bad az faaty
3 " Dyd kh naznyn mah pykr az ps prdh pyda fhd knyzy dr pyfh au
4 " Shmaa bdft grfth amd u dr pyfh rftm nfhft-*Nzm*-zprdh bramd yky
5 " Mahruy :: chu khurfhyd taban pr az rnk u buy."

THROUGHOUT this fpecimen, it is to be obferved, that the diacritical points of *pa*, as in the firft word, and of *Shin*, as in the third and fourth words, are blended together and confufed: over *Ruftam*, the fecond word in the fecond line, is the mark *Damma*, giving the found of *o* or *u*; the points of *ta*, in *Ruftum*,

Kefteranced,

Kefteraneed, Saaty, &c. are blended into one; and the points of *ba, fa, za, Nun*, &c. are out of proportion, large, as in the words *Az, Sheb*, and *Guzafht*, of the firft line, and, in almoft every other word, where fuch letters occur. Over the word *Khaüb*, in the 2d line, is written *Shud*, which, feemingly, the writer had omitted. In the word *Peikur*, (3d line) a long unmeaning ftroke unites the letters *Ya* and *Caf*. The ftroke of *Shin* in *Shud*, (3d line) is thrown over part of the preceding word *Peida*. In *Keneezy* (3d line) the *Nun, Ya*, and *Za*, are run into each other without much diftinction. In *Bedoft* (4th line) the point under *Ba*, is fo large, as to appear like two blended together, and in the word *Nifheft*, (4th line) the points of *Nun* and *Shin*, are not in their proper fituations. Of *Khorfheed*, (5th line) the laft fyllable is thrown above the line, and the point of *Kha*, being placed at the left, feems to belong to the *Ra*. The *Nun*, of *Runk*, in the laft line, is not placed exactly over its letter; and all the final *Yas* in this fpecimen, are defcribed without their points.

OF the great Ruftam, already mentioned, the gallant actions and wonderful exploits conftitute a very confiderable part of the celebrated Heroic Poem by *Ferdufi*, intitled the *Shah Nameh*, or Book of Kings; from a manufcript abridgement

CHAP. V.] PERSIAN MISCELLANIES. 113

ment of that work in profe and verfe, the fpecimen above given is extracted; relating an amorous adventure of a very fingular and romantic nature.

It is there told, that, after a fumptuous feaft, and magnificent entertainment, given in honour of Ruftam, by the King of Sitemgàm*, to which wine and mufic contributed all their charms, a couch or bed being carefully prepared for the Perfian hero, he retired to reft; and after a fhort time was aftonifhed at the appearance of a lovely damfel, who advanced from behind the curtains or hangings†. Her face was beautifully ferene and fair as the filver-moon; yet dazzling like the Sun from its exquifite beauty and glowing complexion: Nor has the poet forgotten thofe delightful odours that her prefence fhed around; perfume being an indifpenfable attribute of complete Perfian elegance.

* This country, as another part of the work informs us, bordered on Turàn, or Turcomania, the Ancient Scythia.

† The ufe of hangings, pictured tapeftry, and various coloured carpets, has been from the earlieft ages prevalent in the Eaft.—We read in the Book of Efther, Chap. I. &c. of the magnificence of a Perfian Monarch, who made a feaft unto his nobles of Perfia and Media, and in his palace had hangings, "white, green, and red," faftened with purple cords to filver rings, with beds of gold and filver, &c. Plutarch, in Themiftocles, fpeaks of the rich Perfian carpets, with highly coloured figures; and in his life of Cato the Cenfor, he mentions fome Babylonian tapeftry, Επιβλημάτων ποικιλων Βαβυλωνιων," fent to Rome as a prefent. The manufacture paffed in very early times from Afia into Greece; part of which, indeed, was itfelf Afiatic. Iris found Helen employed on figured tapeftry; and the web of Penelope is fufficiently known. Iliad III.

Q   This

This fair Princess informs Ruſtam, that ſhe had choſen that hour to come alone and unperceived: that ſhe was daughter of the King of Sitemgaũn, had heard of Ruſtam's wonderful actions and excellent qualities, and that ſhe had made a ſolemn vow, never to beſtow her hand on any other man. The ſecluſion of females in the Eaſtern Countries, from the converſation of men, will, in ſome meaſure, account for the abrupt manner in which the fair one diſcloſed her paſſion, and for her ſeizing on ſuch an opportunity, to obtain an interview with the object of her admiration. But the acknowledgement of her love was delivered in terms ſo ſimple and modeſt, her conduct ſo guarded, and her demeanour ſo correct, that Ruſtam was leſs affected by the ſplendour of her beauty, than filled with reſpect for her candour, her innocence, and virtue*.

OF

* Near the ruined Palace of Perſepolis, now called *Chehel minaũr*, are ſhewn the gigantic figure of a Warrior, and that of a Female, who hold between them each with one hand, ſomething of an annular form, but proportionably large enough to go round the neck: to theſe figures Tradition has beſtowed the name of Ruſtam, and of his favourite Miſtreſs, probably the fair Princeſs of Sitemgaũn. If we can judge from the drawings of M. Le Bruyn, (a painter by profeſſion) the figure of the Warrior expreſſes manly ſtrength, and that of the Princeſs is not inelegant, either in point of attitude or drapery.— Le Brun's Travels in Muſcovy, Perſia, &c. and Kæmpfer, ſpeaking of this ſculpture ſays, " Hæc, venuſta humanæ ſtaturæ femina, fonte redimiculâ, occipite cincinnis, collo mo-
" nili, multis quaſi unionibus bullato ornata eſt, &c."—Amænit. Exoticæ. P. 363.

A Caſhmerian

CHAP. V.] PERSIAN MISCELLANIES. 115

OF this myſterious interview, and the ſubſequent union of our hero with the Princeſs, the reſult was a ſon, whom the King, her father, educated after Ruſtam's departure, and called by the name of *Sohraûb*. The youth having learned from his mother the ſtrange circumſtances of his birth, and of Ruſtam's fame, reſolved to ſet out in queſt of adventures, and immediately commenced a ſeries of brave and gallant actions. But being ſo unfortunate as to encounter his own father, each ignorant of his relation to the other, the iſſue of the combat proved fatal to *Sohraûb*, who did not, however, expire, until it was diſcovered that he fell by a parent's hand. The circumſtances attending this diſcovery, the dying words and filial affection of the ill-fated youth, and the father's vehement affliction and diſtreſs, afford the Poet *Ferduſi*, a fine ſubject for many intereſting and beautiful paſſages in that Chapter, of which I have given the title in the Fourth Number of the Fifth Plate.

A Caſhmerian writer of diſtinction, deſcribing the deſart between Herat and Balkh, ſpeaks of the Travels of Ruſtam as we do of Cyrus's, or of Cæſar's. " Ruſtam, the ſon of Zal, " ſays he," marched by this road from Iraûn to Turan."—See the Memoirs of Khojeh Abdulkerum, tranſlated from the Perſian, by Mr. Gladwin. P. 36. 1793.

Q 2 CHAP.

CHAPTER VI.

PLATE VII. No. 1.

" *Chu Dara javab-i-Skander sheneed.*"
" When Darius heard the anfwer of Alexander."

THIS line is here given merely to illuftrate a remark on the little character which in fome manufcripts is ufed to diftinguifh a Noun governing a Genitive Cafe.—See Chap. IV.

THIS mark is found under the word *javab*, (anfwer) and while in pronunciation it gives the fhort found of *e*, *i*, or *a*, it correfponds in fignification with our prepofition *of*.

THE original order of letters in this line is:

" *Chu Dara juab Skndr shnyd.*"

THE points of the firft letter (Chim) are not diftinctly marked; and the laft word *Sheneed*, is partly thrown above the preceding word, *Skander*.

I CAN-

Plate VII.

| شراب از دوست خوبان سلسبیلست | چو دارا جواب سکندر شنیده |

کنیزی سیه چشم و پاکیزه‌رویی ۰۰ گل اندام و نسکر لب و مشکبوی

ز یونانیان ارغنون زن بسی ۰۰ که نزد ومه بستاند از دل هر کسی

کیست این لعبت خندان که پری‌وش داریم ۰۰ الغرض قرار از دل دیوانه سبک‌بار ببرد

باغ عمر ا مبادو خزان ۰۰ شاخ عمری نوامین از فرخند

CHAP. VI.]   PERSIAN MISCELLANIES.   117

I CANNOT pafs to the next number of this plate, without offering one obfervation on the fubject of the proper names, which occur in the fpecimen before us: (a line from the *Skander Nameh*); it is to point out the reciprocal corruption of thofe proper names by the Greeks and Perfians: each adapting the foreign word to their own idiom or conception of foft-pronunciation.

THUS of the Perfian *Dara* the Greeks have formed *Dareios* and the Macedonian Hero is called *Skander* by the Perfians, or *Ifkander*, the word being often written with an initial *Alif*.

WHY the Perfians have fuppreffed the *l* in *Alexander*, it would be vain, I believe, to inquire, but their alphabet not furnifhing any fingle character correfponding with the harfh ξ, it was natural to adopt the letters *K* and *S*, as a combination that neareft expreffed the found of the Greek confonant, and thefe letters they have accordingly made ufe of " *per* " *Metathefin*."

FOR the fame reafon the Italians write *Aleffandro*; and the rejected ξ is properly changed into *S* or *Sh*; for Etymologifts derive it from the Hebrew שׁ *Shin*, and it often correfponds with ס the letter *Samech*, as in the word סײף: (a fword), from the Chaldaic סיפא *Seiphâ* (a fword.)

AND altho' the Grecians latterly ufed this letter to exprefs the *S* or *Sh* of other nations, as *Roxana* for the Perfian *Rufhenk*,

Rufkenk, &c, yet it is probable that in pronunciation the difference was not perceptible: for the letter ξ was altogether unknown to the very ancient Greeks, and only partially received by the moderns; the Dorics ufed it in fome few inftances for *Sigma*, the Attics were very late in adopting it, and it never found its way into the Æolic dialect*.

But I fhall here clofe my obfervations on this fubject: as I defign in a future work (for which I have already compiled a confiderable ftock of materials) to publifh fome remarks on the collateral affinity of the Greek and Perfian languages, as derived from the Hebræo-Chaldaic.

PLATE VII. No. 2.

" *Shraub az doft-e khoobaun Selfebeel eft,*"

"Wine from the hands of lovely cup-bearers is like the
" celeftial waters of Selfebeel (a fountain in Paradife)."

* See the " Cadmus Græco-Phœnix, of the learned Martinius, p. 1153; and the Hierozoicon, of Bochart, Vol. I. p. 507. The letter ξ had the fame numerical value as the *Sam-ch* of the Hebrews, and the Æolian Greeks, like the Perfians, in the name of Alexander, expreffed it by *K* and *S*, thus they wrote μϙαξι for αϙαξ, and by a Metathefis of thofe letters σκιν⊛ for ξινος.

Befides the principal dialects of ancient Greece, there were innumerable fubordinate idioms and local peculiarities in fpeech; thus in the Ifland of Crete alone, it is faid that there were no lefs than ninety; and the fame words, uttered by a Lacedemonian, would be fcarcely underftood by the more refined inhabitant of Athens.—See Gul. Burton Græcæ Ling. Hift. London, Duod. 1657. p. 27 and 30.

CHAP. VI.]   PERSIAN MISCELLANIES.   119

THERE are not in this fpecimen any difficulties which the following mode of writing will not, I believe, explain,

" Shrab az dft khuban Sljbyl'ft."

THE points of the firft letter *Shin* are confufed; the final *Nun* in *Khoobaun* wants its diacritical point, and over that word is thrown the beginning of the laft word Selfebeel.

WINE, at all times grateful to the Perfians, becomes doubly acceptable, when prefented by the hand of a lovely cup-bearer. We accordingly find that of the lyric compofitions of Hafiz, Jamì, Sadi, and others, many begin with an addrefs to the *Sawky*, or young perfon, whofe office is to fill the goblets, and prefent them to the guefts. I have given, in another part of this work, an extract from one of Sadi's Odes, in which he fays, that, " the cup, if touched by the lips of the fair nymph " who offers it, would overflow with the fweeteft beverage :" here the fame poet affirms, " that the juice of the grape, would " affume a divine nature, if prefented by a beautiful attendant ;" for the fountain *Selfebeel*, is one of thofe, fuppofed to rife in the garden of celeftial Paradife.

" How

"How can wine," (fays *Jami*, in a fonnet addreffed to his miftrefs) "though forbidden on every other occafion, be deem-"ed unlawful, when offered by thy hand?"

"*Shraub' ra keh be her jaw haràm midarend,*
"*Agher az deft-i too bafhud haràm chun gùeem.*"

AND the poet *Khofrù*, in his Divaun, fays, that, "if he "could find but fome drops of wine in the cup which had "been touched by the lips of his beloved, he could with thofe, "as with a powerful charm, induce the moft religious men to "forget their vows of abftinence, and indulge in the forbidden "joys of wine."

"*Juraat gher biyabem az leb-i too,*" &c.

THE Perfians, from the earlieft ages, luxurious, and devoted to convivial pleafures, have not been prevailed on by the precepts of the Koran, nor influenced by the example of the more auftere Arabians, to abftain from wine, which their country in general, and efpecially the province of Shirauz, produces in abundance, and of moft excellent quality: (See Chapter II. p. 26;) to this all travellers bear witnefs, and particularly the German Ambaffadors, who were fent from the Duke of Holftein, into Perfia, about the year 1637: they delight in defcribing the frequent entertainments, and drunken feafts to which they were invited, and the wine they received in prefents:

CHAP. VI.]   PERSIAN MISCELLANIES.   121

fents: they relate alfo the death of one courtier, in confequence of exceffive drinking*.

A CELEBRATED Italian traveller, a little before that time, fpeaking of the Perfians, declares, that they never fail at quaffing excellent wine, " *e fi fta bene fpeffo a tavola della matina infin' alla fera bevendo fempre vino e chi più ne bee è più galant- huomo,*" &c. "and they often," he adds, "remain at table from morning till night, and he who fwallows moft of it, is reckon- ed the fineft fellow†." Indeed, if we may believe another ingenious European, who feems perfectly acquainted with the manners and difpofition of the Perfians, thofe only abftain from wine, who cannot afford the means of indulging in it, and are indebted to indigence alone, for their reputation of fobriety‡.

IN the courfe of this work, the reader will find fome other extracts and obfervations on the fame fubject. I fhall only remark, in this place, that in the Dictionaries, there are found above an hundred words (Perfian and borrowed from the Ara- bic) to exprefs wine, and its derivatives.

* See the " Travels of the Ambaffadors, &c." By Olearius.
† " Viaggi di Pietro della Valle," p. 290. Quarto, Rome, 1658.
‡ Angelo's " Gazophylacium Perficum," p. 397.

R   PLATE

PLATE VII. No. 3.

" *Keneezy feyah-chefhm, va pakeezeh rooee,*
" *Gulendaum va fheker-leb, va Mufhke-booee.*"

" A damfel, black-ey'd, and fair-faced,
" (With) rofy cheeks, fugar'd lips, and mufky fragrance."

In the word *Keneezy*, the medial *Ya* is fcarcely marked by any indenture, and the fame may be obferved of the *Ya* in *Pakeezeh*. The final *Ya* in *Keneezy*, and thofe at the end of both lines, want their diacritical points. The *Za* of *Keneezy*, and of *Pakeezeh*, is to be known merely by its point. In the word *Chefhim*, the ftroke of *Shin* is a continuation of the lower ftroke of *Chim*, without any diftinction. In the hollow of *Gaf* in *Gul*, is placed the *Alif* of *Endaùm*: and the laft word *Mufhkbooee*, is begun above the line, and over the preceding *Waw*, which itfelf is irregularly thrown above the word *Leb*. Thefe lines, are thus written in the original fpelling:

" *Knyzy fyh chfhm u pakyzh ruy,*
" *Gl audam u fhkrlb u mfhkbuy.*"

Between the lines are placed thofe little reverfed commas; figures, which, as I before remarked, are ufed to diftinguifh poetry when it follows profe.

AMONG

CHAP. VI.] PERSIAN MISCELLANIES.

AMONG the chief beauties of the Persian language, is the very great facility with which compound adjectives may be formed, " in the variety and elegance of which," (to use the words of Sir William Jones*) " it surpasses not only the Ger- " man and English, but even the Greek ;" and the five compound epithets, that occur in the specimen before us, will, in some measure, illustrate the observations of that excellent grammarian, on the application of such compounds by the Persian poets. The first expresses the general taste of the Asiatics, in their admiration of black, or dark-coloured eyes, which, in their descriptions of a perfect beauty, are almost always enumerated among the most powerful and striking charms. The poet *Hafiz*, of *Shirauz*, in the last couplet of a beautiful sonnet, uses the epithet, *Seyah-cheshm*, in the plural, as a substantive, and boasts that " his poetry occasioned festivity " and smiles among the black-eyed nymphs of *Cashmere*, and the lovely maids of *Samarcand*†.

" *Az*

---

* Jones's Pers: Grammar, third Edit. p. 70 and 79.

† The sonnet, from which this passage is taken, and the elegy quoted in page 76, have never publicly appeared in a translation ; indeed, of the poems which compose the Divaûn, of *Hafiz*, that most excellent of lyric poets, although they amount in number to nearly six hundred, scarce thirty, as I believe, have yet been published, with a version, in any European tongue : an edition of this celebrated poet's works, to be comprised in one folio volume, was undertaken at Calcutta, in the beginning of the year 1790, containing the original Persian text, and an introductory account of *Hafiz* : in the year 1771, the Baron Reviczky.

"*Az shaar-'e Hafiz i Shirauz mikhendend va mireckfend*
"*Seyah-cheshmauni Cashmeery va turkaun-e Samarcandy.*"

And in the first line of another Ode, he exclaims,

"*Mera muhur Seyah-cheshmaun ze dil biroon nekhabed shud.*"

"The impression which black-eyed damsels have made on my heart, will never be effaced."

The word *Hawer*, or *Hour*, in the Arabic language, signifies a beautiful woman's fine black-eye; and thence have the virgins of Paradise derived their name*. In short, among the eastern writers, the epithet "*Black-eyed*," seems to be synonymous with "*beautiful*†."

Reviczky, published at Vienna, in one volume, octavo, sixteen of his odes, with a Latin translation, prose and verse, under the title of "*Specimen Poeseos Persicœ*, &c." a learned and valuable work, extremely rare; from which Mr. Richardson chiefly formed his "*Specimen of Persian Poetry*," in one volume, quarto, 1774, containing three of the odes, with an English paraphrase in verse, a literal prose translation, and several excellent notes; and Mr. Nott, his "*Select Odes from the Persian Poet, Hafiz*, &c." quarto, 1787; but the most happy translations of this poet's works, are scattered through the writings of Sir William Jones, his "*Histoire de Nader Chah*," in French, quarto, and in English, octavo, 1773; his Persian Grammar, his Latin Commentaries on Asiatic poetry, octavo, 1774, and his "*Poems and Translations from the Asiatic Languages*, octavo. (second edition) 1777.

* See the Koran, Chap. of the mountain, the judgement, the merciful, &c.

† The women use artificial means to give a dark appearance to their eyes; a French traveller informs us, that they set little value on blue, grey, or hazel eyes; the black alone is admired among the Persians.—" Les yeux bleûs, gris ou cendrez ne font pas " les plus beaux felon elles, ce font les noirs."—Sanfon Voyage de Perfe. 91. Duod. 1695.

CHAP. VI.]   PERSIAN MISCELLANIES.   125

The Greeks, like the Perſians, were fond of employing the Roſe in the formation of epithets applicable to beauty. I have before obſerved (ſee the Introduction) the eſteem in which that ſweet flower was held by the ancients.

Anacreon, in a delightful ode, expreſsly written in praiſe of the Roſe, enumerates ſeveral familiar compound epithets in which the Poets uſe it.

"Ροδοδακτυλ☼ μεν Ηως,"
"Ροδοπηχεες δε Νυμφαι"
"Ροδοχρως δε Αφροδιτα," &c.*

"Roſy-fingered Aurora; Nymphs with roſy arms; and roſy "complexioned Venus," &c.

The epithet here applied to the Nymphs, "Roſy "armed," may perhaps, ſeem a little ſtrange to the Engliſh reader, but in Perſian he will find many equally diſagreeing with his idea of beauty; as "Mah-rooee," Moon-faced, &c. an epithet for which I believe, few of our fair countrywomen would thank a lover, although a Perſian miſtreſs would be highly flattered by its application. Thus the poet *Anvàri* uſes it in a paſſage of his Divaùn, where he deſcribes a favourite and beautiful damſel, as "reſembling the grace-

† Anacreon, Ode 55.

"ful

"ful Cyprefs in perfon, with a face lovely as the moon, legs fair as polifhed filver, and rofy check'd."

"*Seroo-ked Mah-e-rooee Seem-fauk va Gul-izaur**."

BUT the Perfian Poets have not an exclufive privilege of ufing thofe flowery compound epithets in their defcriptions of beauty; the writers of profe, indulge to excefs in the application of them: thus in an original and curious romance, now before me, a wandering Dervifh, in the relation of his adventures, defcribes a certain palace, into which he entered, and beheld a gallery or falloon, full of the moft lovely females, —" beautiful European idols,"† all with faces dazzling as the " fun, ferene as the moon, elegant in perfon; with bofoms " fragrant as jeffamine; with flowing ringlets defcending to " their waifts; all like Venufes of Cheen (or Tartary)—fo " beautiful as to excite the envy of the moon; lovely crea-" tures, the delight of the heart, graceful in ftature, rofy

---

* I have already mentioned (p. 19.) and not without a difgraceful infinuation, the Divaun of the ancient and excellent *Anvari*: a work almoft totally unknown to Europeans, though honourably quoted by the firft writers of the Eaft.

† The word *Senem* and *Butt*, are ufed by the Perfians in their amorous compofitions, to exprefs the objeƈt of their love and adoration, as the Italians ufe the word *Idol*, on the fame occafion.

CHAP. VI.]   PERSIAN MISCELLANIES.   127

" cheeked and moon-faced, with looks like the timid glances
" of the fawn*; black eye lashes, softly-closed lips; necks
" fair as silver, with ringlets dark and fragrant as musk,
" forming snares; mouths like the buds of roses, accents elo-
" quent and sweet."

This description, in the original, is a continued string of epithets; which it would be impossible to translate literally into any European language without gross barbarisms, as the Persian scholar will be convinced of, on reading the following lines, containing the passage, as in the manuscript†.

" *Nazuneen senemaun Feringy, hemeh khorsheed leka, va hemeh meh-*
" *peiker, hemeh nazuk endam, va hemeh seemeen ber, va hemeh keisoy*
" *diraz va hemeh mooee kemer, hemeh zehreh Cheen va hemeh rishk kumr,*
" *nazuneen dilaramy, nazuk endamy, gulizaur, mah-e-rokhsaury, ahu-*
" *negahy, mezkàn seyahy, besteh leby, seem-ghebguhy, mushkeen mooey,*
" *kumend keifooy, ghuncheh dehauny, shireen zubauny.*"

---

* The *Ahu*, which I have translated *fawn*, according to a learned naturalist (Kœmpfer Amen. Exot. p. 404) differs only from the Stag in being bearded and having horns without branches; the fullness and sweetness of this creature's eye, are subjects of innumerable allusions among the Persian Poets in their descriptions of female beauty.

† A large Octavo volume, entitled the " Kisseh chehar Dervish" or Romance of the Four Dervises,"—an ingenious and entertaining collection of narratives, interspersed with fragments of poetry, gazels, or short sonnets, quotations from Hafez, and other poets, &c.

OF

OF the epithet, expressing a musky odour, used, as in the specimen, by the poet *Nezami*, and in the prose passage just quoted, I shall remark, that costly and most exquisite perfumes are esteemed the first among Asiatic luxuries; musk, ambergris, and the wood of aloes, generally form part of the magnificent offerings from one prince to another*. So fond of aromatic and highly fragrant ointments were the ancients, that many writers have made their excessive indulgence in the use of perfumes, the subject of learned dissertations†, and this, like a rivulet from its fount, and many other branches of Asiatic effeminacy, flowed through the surrounding nations, and found their way even into Greece and Rome, from Persia, or Assyria, the great source of Eastern luxury and refinement‡.

AMONG the sensual delights of the Mahometan Paradise, we learn from the Korân, that musk is to contribute its power-

* See " Mirchond's Historia Priorum Regum Persarum, Note, p. 134. 4to. Vienna. 1782, and Gladwin's Narrative of the Transactions in Bengal, p. 53, 56, &c. 8vo. Calcutta, 1788.

† Caufabon, Demster, Rhodiginus, and others, quoted by *Martin Geier*, in his Treatise " de Ebræorum luctu," third edition, duod. Franc. 1683. p. 395, where he speaks of the luxuries of the Greeks, Syrians, Babylonians, &c.

‡ The fashion of several garments, and the use of costly ornaments, were borrowed from the Asiatics, by the ancient Grecians. " At non intra solos Orientis fines mos " gestandi compedes, se continuit, sed in Græciam quoque emanavit ; nempe ut sequentia " pluribus docebunt, magna luxus et Vestium Orientalium pars ex Persia ad Græcos " perlata." Schræderi Comment. de Vestitu Mulierum Hebræarum, published by Schultens, 4to. Leyden, 1745, p. 14.

ful

ful odour, for with that fragrant fubſtance, are to be ſeal'd the veſſels containing the celeſtial beverage of the faithful, that wine which is to recompenſe the pious muſulman for his abſtinence in this tranſitory ſtate. "*Khatema'ho miſkon*," &c. (See the Koran, Chap. 83, verſe 26.)

I HAVE already mentioned (p. 62,) the high eſteem in which thoſe perfumes are held by the Aſiatics. I ſhall, in this place only remark, that however fond the Perſians may be of the ſweet fragrance of the roſe and jeſſamine, the ſtronger odours of muſk and ambergris, are ſtill with them the favourites of the toilet. Theſe among us, are now but little uſed for the purpoſes of perfume; muſk has long been ſupplanted by the milder vegetable preparations, the animal fragrance being uſed only in medicinal compoſitions: " It is thus, ſays Goldſmith," (ſpeaking of thoſe perfumes no longer faſhionable, though once regarded as eſſential to elegance,) " that things which become neceſſa-
" ry, ceaſe to continue pleaſing, and the conſciouſneſs of their
" uſe, deſtroys their power of adminiſtering delight*.

* Goldſmith's Hiſtory of the Earth and Animated Nature. Muſk animal, vol. 3.

PLATE VII. No. 4.

" *Z'yunaniaùn organoon-e zun pefy*
" *Keh burdeud hoofh az dil-e her kefy.*"

" OF the Grecians were many performers on the organ, who deprived of
" underſtanding the minds of every one."

IN this ſpecimen it is to be remarked, that the points of medial *ya* are blended together: that final *ya* is deſcribed without points; that the final *nun* of *Organoon* having been omitted in its proper place, is written below the line, and that the points of all the letters are thrown very high above or below the line. In the ſecond line three different figures of the letter *ha* occur, which the following letters will point out.

" Z'yunanyan argnun zn pſy,
" Kh brdnd huſh az dl hr kſy.

OVER *burdend* is placed the orthographical mark *damma* giving the ſound of *o* or *u*: and under the word *dil*, is placed another, *Cafra*, giving that of *i* or *ee*, and denoting that a genitive

CHAP. VI.] PERSIAN MISCELLANIES.

genitive cafe follows " *dil-i-herkefy, the heart of every one.*" Each member of the couplet is feparated from the other by a ruled line (which is generally of red or blue ink, fometimes of gold) the work being all verfe, from which the fpecimen is given. Little figures like commas, as in the laft Number, diftinguifh verfes when fcattered through profe.

THE powers of mufic, which have been felt and acknowledged in all ages, and in every country, have never, perhaps, been fo well defcribed as in that admirable compofition of Dryden, in which we read of its wonderful effects at

" The Royal Feaft for Perfia won,
" By Philip's warlike fon."

THE fpecimen before is extracted from the *Skander-Nameh* or hiftory of Alexander, the warlike fon of Philip, where, defcribing a truly royal feaft, the poet Nazami, enumerates the various forts of mufical inftruments, peculiar to feveral nations, which were collected there, and contributed their harmony to the delights of this very fplendid entertainment. I have felected from the original paffage, that line which
mentions

132	PERSIAN MISCELLANIES.	[CHAP. VI.

mentions the organs of the *Ionians* or Greeks* and the skill of the performers on that instrument, which " ravished the senses of all that heard its tones."

WHATEVER may be the instrument, here called by the name of *Aurganoon*, the following extract from a Persian Lexicon, will shew the high opinion entertained of it by the Asiatics, who ascribe its invention to one of the greatest Philosophers of ancient Greece.

" *Aurganoon, Organè, &c. naum-e-sauzy est keh Aflatoon wasia est*
" *wa akser u agleb Roomiaun u Nazary darend.*"

" ORGANOON, &c. the name of a musical instrument which
" Plato invented, and which is chiefly in use among the Europeans
" and Christians."

IT is, I fear, almost impossible to ascertain what may have been the authorities of our Persian poet, in his description of the

---

* It appears to me that the word *Ionaun*, for *Grecians*, (like a multitude of other Persian words) has continued unaltered since the days of Aristophanes. In his Greek *Iaonau* the letter *u* may have inadvertently been written for *n* or this letter omitted by the scribes, after the former ; but without correction or alteration, the Greek word exactly expresses the same broad termination of many Persian plurals, with those given by an old Grammarian, who uses *Ademaa*, or *Ademon*, from *Adem*, a man ; *Onaa* from *On* (*ann*) that ; *Inaa* from *In* (*een*) this, &c. I shall take a future occasion to dwell on the subject of this note, and refer the reader to Aristophanes's play " ΑΧΑΡΝΗΣ, Act. 1. Sc. 3. and to
" Father Ignatius's Gram : Ling : Persica, 4to. Rome, 1661, p. 11, 22, 26.

royal

CHAP. VI.]   PERSIAN MISCELLANIES.   133

royal feaſt; he boaſts in the introduction to his hiſtory, that he compiled it from the various works, in different languages, on the ſubject of his hero, Alexander: " I augmented it," he ſays, " from the chronicles of Jews, Chriſtians, and Pehla-" vians ; I ſelected, from each volume, the moſt curious " paſſages ; from every nut-ſhell, I extracted the kernel, and " from the whole, I formed this treaſury of a compilation*." I ſhall not here attempt to enquire into the poet's meaning, in the paſſage juſt quoted; nor ſhall I, in this place, offer any conjectures on thoſe works, to which he alludes, written in the Hebrew, Greek, or Latin, and ancient Perſian tongues, for ſuch I preſume, he means, by *Yehoody*, *Nazrany*, and *Pehlavi*.

THAT Alexander delighted in muſic, we learn from the hiſtorians of Greece and Rome; Timotheus accompanied him into Perſia, and charmed him with his Phrygian airs; he made his female captives ſing to him after their manner, &c. &c. But I ſhall not here encroach on the department of the antiquary, nor anticipate ſome hiſtorical obſervations, which I purpoſe offering in a future work.

* See ſome obſervations on this Work, in p. 78, Chapter V.

PLATE

PLATE VII. No. 5.

" *Keeſt aun laâbet-i-khendaun keh perivar bereſt,*
" *Keh krawr az dil-e deewaneh biyekbar bereſt.*"

" Who is that ſmiling charmer that moved by like an angel, ſo that tranquillity
" at once fled from each diſtracted heart?"

Thus written, according to the original orthography :

" Kyſt anlabt khndan kh pry uar brſt,
" Kh krar az dl dyuanh bykbar brſt."

In this diſtich, the reader will remark, that the points of final *ta*, in the firſt word, are placed at the extremity of that letter, though generally we find them in the centre. The point of *Nun*, in the ſecond word *Aun*, is above the letter: that of final *Nun*, in *Khendaun*, in the center of it. The points of *pa* in *Peri*, are much below the line, and the word *Bereſt*, both in the firſt and ſecond lines is divided, and partly written above the line. The ſtroke of *Caf* in the firſt word of the ſecond line, is drawn acroſs the red ruling, which divides the members of couplets from each other.

OF

Plate VIII.

No. 1
بهار خوش است ای گل کجایی ∥ همه سی بلبلان نالہ و سوز

No. 2
برف پرید نشیند برسرم ∥ عجبنان طبع جوانی میکنہ

No. 3
نغمہ مطرب خوشکو همہ نیست کدام ∥ ساغر می ساقی مہ وجہ فتنہ گشا

No. 4
ساقی سیمین جنبی خیز ∥ آب شا دی بر آتش غم ریز
بوسہ بر کنار نغز زن ∥ پس بگیر دان شراب شعاع انگیز

No. 5
ساقیا وصل بہ از نو مبارک باشد

No. 6
بر آمد باد صبح و بوی نوروز

Chap. VI.] PERSIAN MISCELLANIES.

OF this couplet, which begins a beautiful fonnet in the Divan of Sâdi, I fhall confine my obfervations to one word, I mean that which I have tranflated, *Angel*, for want of a better term to exprefs my idea of the Perfian *Peri*, a being, which as I already obferved*, may be ftyled the faireft creature of poetical imagination; but of which, I have never feen, nor indeed, is it reafonable to expect, any fatisfactory definition.

FOR on the fubject of fictitious beings, as every perfon is at liberty to form what idea will moft pleafe, fo we might naturally expect to find various opinions, entertained by the poets of the Peri fpecies.

WITHOUT deftroying the general and principal characteriftics of gods and goddeffes, the Greek and Roman poets, affign to each, properties and attributes, as beft fuit the immediate purpofe of their poems: and we accordingly find fcarce any of the claffical divinities free from fome degrading ftain. Their celeftial minds were actuated by the moft irregular paffions, they were vindictive, cruel, and unrelenting in their anger†, and guilty of every debauchery and fcandalous excefs, that could difgrace even mortals.

BUT the Perfian Peries, however vaguely defined as to fpecies and appearance, are uniformly defcribed, as beneficent,

---

* See " Introduction."
† " Tantæne animis celeftibus iræ." Virg.

beautiful.

beautiful, and mild; and if the elegant Marmontel*, had reason to lament the decline of the Fairy Syſtem among us, ſurely the abſence of the Perſian Peries, is much more to be regretted; of whom, none were miſchievous or malignant, like many of the Fairies, none deformed or diminutive; but all ſo amiable in diſpoſition, and ſo lovely in aſpect, as to be the direct contraſt, or oppoſite to the *Dives*, a race of cruel, hideous, and wicked creatures of the imagination, as oppoſite as vice and virtue, or any qualities perfectly incompatible†. Thus the poet *Jami*, expreſſes his aſtoniſhment, that, "one of thoſe evil ſpirits could be an inmate with a *Peri*."

"*Keh deewy ba Peri hemkhàneh baſhy.*"

NOTWITHSTANDING this excellence of their nature, the Perſian Peries ſeem to be a diſtinct ſpecies of imaginary beings, and I know not any claſs of airy creatures, in which they can, with exact propriety be ranked.

* "J'ai grand regret à la feerie, c'etoit pour les imaginations vive une ſource des "plaiſirs innocens, et la maniere la plus honnête de faire d'agrèables ſonges, &c. &c." See Marmontel's Contes Moraux, Alcidonis.

† On the ſubject of the Dives, I have offered ſome remarks, in the account of Ruſtam's combat with the Dive Sepeed, given in the Explanation of No. 1, Plate VI. Although I have there ſaid, in general terms, that the Peries were females, yet there are a few exceptions; Mr. Richardſon, in his Diſſertation, mentions one, and in a manuſcript before me, the words, *Murd*, a man, and *Peri*, are indifferently uſed, in deſcribing the apparition of an aerial ſpirit.

HOWEVER

CHAP. VI.]   PERSIAN MISCELLANIES.   137

However they may correspond in beauty with our idea of angels, they cannot well be supposed those beings whom the Hebrews called מלאך, and the Greeks Αγγελος; since of both words, the theme is " to send," for the Peries are not commissioned from above on any occasion; besides, the Persians have the term, " *Ferishteh**," to express the distinct race of angels, or heavenly messengers.

They cannot be classed among the שרפים " the rapt Seraph " that adores and burns ;" nor among the כרובים " winged " Cherubs," for they are not said to have any place in heaven. There is also another species of rational creatures, whom the Ancient Hebrews, called *Shedeem*, שדים but with whom the Peries do not exactly correspond; they, in some respects, resembled angels, having wings, and a knowledge of future events, and were but too like the human race, in requiring substantial food, and being mortal†. Nor do the Peries answer to those intelligences whom, the Platonics called *Dæmons*, from Δαιμων, *Sciens*, *Wise*, &c. nor to the Genii of the Romans, who watched over mortals, given from their birth (*à gignendo*) into their charge; nor are they by any means those celestial virgins, whose charms are to reward the pious musulman in a future state, and whom the Arabs call " *Houri*." Yet, those gentle

* From " *Ferishaden*," to send.
† Millii Diss. de Mohammedismo, &c. p. 15. The word *Shedeem*, is found only in the plural. See Pagninus's Thesaurus Ling. Sanctæ."

T   beings,

beings, poffeffing exquifite beauty, the poet *Sadi*, knows not, "whether his miftrefs be an Houri of Paradife, an angel, a "daughter of man, or a Peri."

"*Houri nedaunem ya mulluk firzendeh audim ya Peri.*"

To continue this negative defcription of the Perfian Peries, I find, that they by no means accord with our Shakfpeare's idea of the Fairy race. However fond they may be of perfumes, (and fragrant odours are their only nourifhment) we do not read of their being employed in

"Killing cankers in the mufk-rofe buds."

Nor of their being compelled

"To ferve the Fairy Queen,
"To dew her orbs upon the green," &c.
"They muft go feek fome dew-drops here and there,
"And hang a pearl in every cowflips ear*."

I cannot difcover, that the Perfian Peries, have ever been fuppofed fo diminutive in ftature, as to "war with Rere mice "for their leathern wings†, to pafs through key-holes‡, or to hide in the bells of flowers§. But the fublime idea, which

---

* Midfummer Night's Dream.   † Ibid.   ‡ Gay's Fable, "The Nurfe and the Fairy."
§ "Where the bee fips, there lurk I,
"In a cowflip's bell I lie, &c."   *Shakfpeare's Tempeft.*

Milton

CHAP. VI.] PERSIAN MISCELLANIES.

Milton entertained of a fairy vifion, correfponds rather with that which the Perfian poets have conceived of the Peries:

" Their port was more than human as they flood——
" ——I took it for a fairy vifion,
" Of fome gay creatures of the element,
" That in the colours of the rainbow live,
" And play in th' plighted clouds—I was awe-ftruck,
" And as I pafs'd, I worfhip'd*."

This fine paffage, gives me, I confefs, a much clearer idea of the light, airy, yet fublimely beautiful Peries, than any other I have met with.

The ingenious Mr Richardfon informs us, that although fuppofed to live very long, the Peries are not faid to be exempt from the common fate of mortals†; their exiftence, probably is not to clofe but with the final diffolution of this univerfe; for if we may believe Ariofto, " No fairy can die " as long as the fun moves round, or the heavens remain in " their prefent ftate."

" Morir non puote alcun' Fata mai,
" Fin ch'l Sol gira o il ciel non muta ftilo‡."

* Milton's Comus.
† Differtation prefixed to the Arab. and Perfian Dict. p. 36.
‡ Orlando Furiofo, Canto x. p. 56.

My obfervations hitherto having tended principally to fhow what the Perfian Peries are not like, I fhall candidly acknowledge my inability of afcertaining what they may be faid to refemble; that exquifite beauty is their moft obvious characteriftic, appears from the poets, who, when they wifh to compliment, in the moft flattering manner, an admired object, compare her to one of this aerial race. I have no doubt that the name is derived (as that of our *Fairy*) from the Hebrew ראפ, beauty, elegance, &c.* and I can venture to affirm that he will entertain a pretty juft idea of a Perfian Pery, who fhall fix his eyes on the charms of a beloved and beautiful miftrefs.

PLATE VII. No. 6.

" *Baug'-i-umretra mebad khuzaùn."—*
" *Shauk-e-umry too aimun az ferghend.*"

" May the garden of thy life, never feel the winds of autumn."
" May the branch of thy tree of life be free from the ivy of decay."

IN the firft word of this example, the tail of final *Ghain* is brought between the initial *ba*, and its point. The three letters

* See " Introduction."

of

CHAP. VI.] PERSIAN MISCELLANIES. 141

of *umr*, in both lines, are fo connected as nearly to render the word perpendicular; the *Ra* in *tira*, is almoſt a continuation of the ſtroke of *ta*, and the *ba* in *mebad*, is to be known merely by its point; the final *nun* in *Khuzaùn*, is very open at the top, and its point thrown high above the line.

In the ſecond line the points of *Shin*, in the firſt word, are confufedly expreſſed, as thofe alfo of *ta* in the word too. In *aimun* the points of *ya* are not exactly under that letter; and that of final *nun* is at a great height above the line. In *ferghund*, the point of *nun* is placed over the laſt letter *Da*; the lines in the original order of words and letters are thus:

" Bagh amr tra mbad khzan"—
" Shakh amry tu aymn az frghnd."

IN the moſt admired ſpecimens of their epiſtolary compofitions, we generally find that the Perſians introduce benedictions fimilar to that given in the annexed plate: and as they are extremely ſtudious of elegant and flowery language, even in the moſt familiar correſpondence, ſeveral ingenious and learned men, have employed their talents in compofing models of letters on various ſubjects, and ſuitable to every claſs and defcription of writers; among thofe, *Herkern* and *Eufoofy*, have compiled the moſt excellent *Infkas*, or forms of letter

letter writing; the *Infsa-i-Herkern* has been publifhed with an Englifh verfion*; that of *Enfofy*, ftill remains in manufcript; from one of the letters in a fine copy of this work now before me, I fhall extract the following couplet, from which, as from the greater number of paffages fcattered through the works of this nature, one would fuppofe that among the Afiatics, longevity was efteemed the greateft bleffing heaven could beftow a friend.

"*Bad jahet bikyas, bad feyfet bikeraun.*"
"*Bad ghurret bee zuwal, va bad umret javedaun.*"

" May you be exalted to a ftation of unbounded dignity!
" May your affluence and profperity be infinite!
" May your dawning morn never fet in night,
" And may thy life be eternal!"

The original beauty of the eaftern benediction given in the fpecimen, has induced me to prefent it to the reader: it is given from a Perfian poet, in a manufcript *Ferhung*, or Dictionary, under the article " *Ferghendeh*," or " *Ferghend*," which fignifies " Ivy." Having mentioned the pernicious quality of this plant, which renders barren, and finally deftroys each tree that it embraces, the Lexicographer quotes the couplet here given, to illuftrate his definition.

* " *Infhai Herkern*," The forms of Herkern, quarto, Calcutta, 1781. by Dr. Francis Balfour, Perfian and Englifh.

PLATE

CHAP. VI.] PERSIAN MISCELLANIES. 143

PLATE VIII. No. 1.

" *Behaur khoormeſt, ay gul kuja'ee-y?*"
" *Keh beeny bulbulânra nauleh ve ſ:oz.*"

" The ſpring is delightful! oh roſe, where haſt thou been? Doſt thou not
" hear the lamentations of the nightingale, on account of thy delay?"

———————

THE reader will remark, that in theſe lines, many letters are repreſented as mere hair-ſtrokes; and that others in their flouriſhes affect a ſtrong and heavy turn. The letters in the original order are as follow:

" Bhar khurmſt ay gl kjayy ;
" Kh byny blblanra nalh u fuz."

THE point of *Ba* in the firſt word is not exactly in its proper place; nor that of *Kha* in the next word, of which the *mſt* riſe above preceding *ra*, in *Kujayy*; the point of *Jim* is thrown to the left of its letter, and the two firſt letters placed over the hook of the preceding *Lam*. In the ſecond line the points of *ba* and *ya*, in *Beeny*, are placed together; and that

of

of *Nun*, not exactly over the body of that letter, which is expressed by a turned stroke running into the flourish of final *ya*. In *Bulbulanrà*, the *ra* is brought in almost a straight line; the *ha* of *Nauleh* is a short turn of the pen; and the stroke of *Sin* in *Suz*, is thrown over the preceding copulative *Waw*. The accents of *Naleh*, are marked by the *Fathas*, placed over that word; and over *Kujayy* in the first line is the mark *Hamza*, denoting the second person singular of a compound preterite.— See Jones's Grammar, p. 11.

IN this Couplet, by the Poet Sàdi, are comprised three of the most favourite subjects of Persian Song; the Delights of Spring, the Beauty and Fragrance of the Rose, and the Melody of the Nightingale. The Rose, as I have before observed, is supposed allegorically to be the mistress of that sweet bird: and the Poet here chides the flower for its late appearance, although, as he says, " the Spring was delightful, and the Nightingale lamenting the absence of the Rose." Among the Persians it has ever been the object of elegant luxury to gather the first rose of spring; to watch its opening, and enjoy its maturer bloom; and to catch the last breath of its departing sweetness. Thus Horace, expressing his dislike to the

CHAP. VI.]   PERSIAN MISCELLANIES.   145

the cuftoms of the Perfians, defires his attendant to feek no longer like them, " the place where might be found the lateft lingering rofe."

" Mitte fectari Rofa quo locorum."
" Sera moretur."

THE Mahometans, and particularly the Turks, entertain a kind of religious veneration for the rofe; they believe that it firft fprang from the fweat of their Prophet, and therefore they fuffer not its leaves to be trampled under foot*. The Ancients afcribed the origin of this fweet flower to the blood of Venus; and to the warmth of her kifs, a modern Latin poet affirms the rofe is indebted for its glowing tints †.

To what has been faid of the Nightingale in a former part of this volume, I fhall add one obfervation: that although the word *Bulbul* is the name of a Bird, not anfwering in every refpect to our Nightingale, yet its voice being of the fame plain-

* " Sed nec Rofarum folia humi jacere patiuntur," &c.—(De Turcis) Aug. Bufbequii. Epift. I.

† " O quoties dixit talis Adonis erat !
" Sed placidam pueri metuens turbare quietem
" Fixit vicinis bafia mille rofis.
" Ecce calent illæ, cupidæque per ora Diones," &c. &c.

Joan. Secundi Baf. I.

U   tive

tive ſtrain, and it reſembling that bird, in the extraordinary circumſtance of ſinging by night, there is no word which can convey a clearer idea of the Perſian *Bulbul*, than that which I have adopted in the tranſlation.

The plaintive melody of this ſweet bird is not, however, in the Eaſt, ſuſpended during the day-time, as in our colder climate: on the contrary, as its love-laboured ſong is heard at the firſt dawn, the Perſians call it the " *Bulbul Suhury*," or Early Nightingale; and " *Taêr Subuh*," or the " Bird of Morn." Even in the Southern parts of Europe, the Nightingale's voice is often heard by day: A very ancient and intereſting French Poet thus begins one of his love-ſongs, or Chanſons:*

" La douce voix du roſignol ſauvage
" Qu'oi nuit & jor cointoier & tentir,
" Me radoucit mon cuer & raſouage, &c." †

Chanſon. XVIII.

---

* Raoul de Coucy, whoſe Hiſtorical Memoirs, publiſhed 1781, in Paris, two volumes, 12mo. form one of the moſt romantic and affecting ſtories of the age of Chivalry. The melancholy concluſion of his amours with the fair but unfortunate Gàbrielle de Vergi, are too well confirmed by authentic and hiſtoric proofs, to allow one's mind the conſolation uſual after peruſing a narrative of fictitious woe.

† " The ſweet voice of the wild Nightingale,"
" Whom I hear by night and day amuſing himſelf and ſinging,"
" Soothes the anguiſh of my heart, and conſoles me," &c.

CHAP. VI.]   PERSIAN MISCELLANIES.   147

AN English traveller of the last century, writing from Shiràuz, seems inspired by the Persian climate, and adopts the flowery language of the country. " The Nightingale," says he, " sweet harbinger of light, is a constant cheerer of these groves: charming with its warbling strains the heaviest soul into a pleasing ecstacy*;" but it is unnecessary to dwell on the charms of "*this feathered voice,*" as it has been styled by the Italians†, and I refer the English reader to the learned Newton's Notes on the Seventh Book of Paradise Lost, where he enumerates the various passages in which the immortal Milton has delighted to celebrate the praises of "*the Solemn Nightingale.*"

PLATE VIII. No. 2.

" *Burf-e-peery mi nesheened ber ser'em,*
" *Hemchunaun tubàa'm juvani mikened.*"

" The snows of age descend upon my head,
." Yet from the gaiety of my disposition I still am young."

* Doctor Fryer's Travels in Persia. 1681. Folio. Page 243.
† " *Una voce pennata.*"

U 2   THE

THE reader who has perufed with attention the obfervations fcattered through the preceding pages, will find, I believe, very little difficulty in analyzing the letters of this fpecimen, which in the original order ftand thus:

" Brf pyry my nſhynd br frm."
" Hmchnan tbaàm Juvany myknd."

In the word *Peery*, the medial *ya* is fcarcely marked by any indenture, and its points are placed along with that of *pa*, written with one inftead of three; the *Sin* in the laft word *Serm*, rifes above the line. In the fecond line the letters *ha*, *mim*, and *chim*, in the firft word, are nearly perpendicularly placed; and one point fupplies the place of three in *chim*; the final *mim* in *Tubaam*, hangs by a turned ftroke from the preceding *ain*. In the word *Juvany*, the point over *Nun*, is its only diftinction. In the laft word, *Mikend*, a long daſh fills up the line, and unites the *n* with the final *d*.

SO unwilling is the Lyrick Sâdi to acknowledge, that his fpirits were impaired by years, that, although hoary Time had fixed his fnowy emblems on the Poet's head, he yet affirms, that

CHAP. VI.]   PERSIAN MISCELLANIES.   149

that from the natural vivacity of his difpofition, he ftill was young. Such was the kind of perfonage Anacreon loved.

"Φιλῶ γεροντα τερπνον, &c."

"Who," he fays, in nearly the words of our Perfian Poet,

"Τρίχας γερῶν μεν εςί,
"Τας δε φρένας νεαζει*."

"Is old indeed, as to his fnowy locks, but young in fpirits and dif-
"pofition."

From this couplet of the Greek Poet, as the learned Dacier has remarked, is borrowed that paffage of Plautus.

"Si albus capillus hic videtur, neutiquam ingenio eft fenex†."

Which may be tranflated nearly, in the words of the Perfian fpecimen before us, as well as of the Greek lines, from which it was originally borrowed.

* Anacreon, Ode xlvii.
† Plaut. Miles Gloriofus, Act. iii. Sc. 1.

PLATE

PLATE VIII. No. 3.

" *Nughmul-e mutreb khooshkaw hemè pend eft ve kulaùm,*
" *Sàghery ſawky mehroo heme futeh eft ve kuſhad.*"

" The melody of the sweet-singing musician is all our care, and the burden of our conversation.
" The goblet of the lovely moon-faced cup-bearer, is our only subject of triumph and cause of exultation."

IN this specimen the reader will observe, that the final *ta* in the first word is expressed by the letter *ha*; that the stroke of *Shin* in *Khooſh*, comes between the *Kha* and its points. In *Hemeh*, are described two forms of *ha*; the points of *pa* in *Pend*, are not exactly under that letter; and the word *Kulaum*, is placed above the line, and over *waw* and *eſt* preceding. In the second line the letter *ra*, in the first word, hangs obliquely from the *Ghain*; and in the word *Mehroo*, the *ra* is a hair-stroke, connected by a turn of the pen with the medial *ha*. In *Hemeh* are described two *ha's*, differing a little from those in the same word, occurring in the first line; the medial *ta* in *Futtehest*, is suddenly joined to the *hha* by a long stroke: over the *ſt* is placed *waw*, and above that copulative is the last word

CHAP. VI.]   PERSIAN MISCELLANIES.   151

word *Kuſhad*, in which the *Caf* is deſcribed with a very long upper ſtroke, the lower one running abruptly into the indentures of *Shin*: the lines are thus written in the original ſpelling:

" Nghmh mtrb khuſhku hmh pnd ſt u klam."
" Sagry ſaky mhru hmh ſthhſt u kſhad."

———

IN this couplet, the poet *Shah Caſsem Anver*, has deſcribed the general taſte of the Perſian voluptuaries, who delight in their feaſts to unite the pleaſures of wine, with the charms of muſic, and to heighten the luxurious enjoyments of the banquet by the preſence of ſome beloved or beautiful object. Whether it be that the climate inſpires a ſuperior degree of voluptuouſneſs, it is certain that in Perſia, ſenſual pleaſures are purſued with greater eagerneſs than in moſt other countries; few tenants of that luxuriant ſoil being unaffected by the ſoft propenſity,—" We are fond of wine," ſays a Perſian poet,[*]— " wanton, diſſolute and with rolling eyes; but who is there " in this city that has not the ſame vices?" and the general diſſipation is thus mentioned by a proſe writer: " They were " immerſed in pleaſure and delight, and were conſtantly " liſtening to the melody of the lute and of the cymbal.[†]"

[*] Quoted in Jones's Perſian Grammar, p. 34.
[†] Ibid, p. 42.

PERSIAN MISCELLANIES. [Chap. VI.

In Anacreon's beautiful ode on the subject of a feast, Bacchus or wine is thus associated with music and with love*.

" Ἱλαροὶ πίωμεν οἶνον,
" Ἀναμελψομεν δε Βάκχον
" Τον εφευρεταν χορεας
" Τον ολα; ποθοῦντα μολπας
" Τον ομοτροπον Ερωτί
" Τον ερωμενον Κυθηρης."

" Let us gaily drink wine, and sing the praises of Bacchus, who " invented the mazy dance, who delights in every kind of music; " him who is congenial with Love, and is so dear to Venus."—

And the poet Hafiz, in a beautiful Sonnet, wonders that a man can ask any greater blessing from fortune, than permission to indulge in wine, and play with the dishevelled ringlets of his mistress.

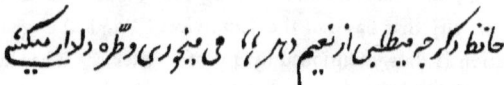

" *Hafiz digur cheh mitulby az naim-i dubur*
" *Meï mikhoory va turreh-e dildar mikushy.*"

* Anacreon, Ode xli.

Those

CHAP. VI.] PERSIAN MISCELLANIES. 153

THOSE who have travelled in Perfia, defcribing feafts and entertainments, relate, that muficians, both vocal and inftrumental, generally attended: that handfome pages carried round the wine, and that finging and dancing women were provided, the venality of whofe charms, befides the exercife of their profeffional talents, completed the luxury of the Perfian banquet.

PLATE VIII. No. 4.

" *Sawkee-i-feemten che khufhy ? k:ez —*
" *Awb-i-fhadee ber 'autifh-i ghum reez,"*
" *Boofeh ber kunar-e faugher zen*,*
" *Pes bekürd aun fheraub fhehed aumeez."*

" Oh cupbearer! with a body fair as filver, why doft thou flumber—arife
" And pour the water of delight on the fire of anguifh:"
" Fix a kifs on the brim of the cup,
" And the wine will then be fweet as if mixed with honey."

IN this fpecimen, which is from a very plain, but fufficiently accurate manufcript, the reader will not perceive any fine hair-ftrokes or flourifhes, or intricate combinations of letters: the four lines as written according to Perfian orthography are

* In one of the MS. copies before me, of Sadi's Divaun, the imperative *Neh*, from *Nehaden*, to place, is ufed inftead of *zen*, from *zeden*, to fix, to ftrike, &c. &c.

" Saky

"Saky fymtn chh khfby khyz,
"Ab fhady br atfh ghm ryz,
"Bufh br knar faghr zn,
"Ps bkrd an fhrab fhhd amyz."

THE firſt word exhibits the letters *Sin* and *Alif*, ſo deſcribed as to form a ſemicircle or bow; the points of *Kaf* and *ya*, (as of *ta*, &c. throughout the ſpecimen) are blended together; the *Sin* of *Seemten* is a very long daſh of the pen, and the *ya* is turned ſuddenly into the *mim*; the final *nun* is very open at the top; *cheh* is expreſſed with only one point for *chim*, and a very ſhort turn for the final *ha*. In *Kheſby* no mark of diſtinction is expreſſed between the *Kha* and *Sin*; the point of *ba* is not exactly under that letter; and in *Kheez*, the middle *ya* is only known by its points; the point of *z* is not in its proper place. As in *Sawky*, of the firſt line, the *Shin* and *Alif* of *Shady* in the ſecond are formed into a ſemicircle; the *ta* of *Auteſh*, has not its points exactly over it, nor are thoſe of *ya* in *Reez* exactly under that letter.

IN the third line, the letters *Sin* and *Ha* of *Booſeh*, are nothing more than a curved ſtroke with a ſhort concluding hairſtroke: in *Kunàr*, the point of *Nun* is over the *Alif*; the *Alif* of *Sagher* ſeems to be only a little upright termination of the *Sin*: the *Ra* is a ſtraight ſtroke proceeding from the lower part of *Ghain*.

CHAP. VI.]   PERSIAN MISCELLANIES.   155

In the fourth line it is to be obferved that the *Shin* of *Shraub*, is expreffed by a very fhort, and flightly indented ftroke; the points confufed; and that over the final *ba* is placed the *Sin* of *Shebed*. In this word, between the *ha* and final *da*, is a long turned ftroke: In *Aumeez*, the medial *ya* is principally diftinguifhed by its points, very little care being taken to exprefs the body of that letter.

ON the compound Epithets of the Perfians, I have already offered fome obfervations: and when the reader, (who may think ftrange that which the Poet Sàdi here ufes, *(Silver-bodied)* recollects thofe which the Grecians applied to admired females, he will be eafily reconciled to the Perfian idiom, which delights in the compofition of fimilar epithets. The Poet here, that he may drown the pangs of grief or trouble, occafioned probably by love, afks the cup bearer for wine, which, by a beautiful Periphrafis, he calls, " the Water of " Gladnefs, or of Joy*." This metaphorical phrafeology, has been, from the earlieft ages, in ufe among the Afiatics:

* The wine touched by his Miftrefs's lips, the Poet fays, will be fweet as if " mixt with honey." It is not improbable, that the Afiatics actually infufe fome fweet fubftances with their wine, and it is certain that the Perfians blend fragrant and aromatic compofitions with their favourite liquors. (See p. 42.) The exceffive luxury of the ancient Greeks in this refpect, is noticed by Ælian, (Lib. xii. Cap. 31). " Τί δε, κχ εκεῖνα τοι. " Ελληνοι τρυφῆς αποδειξις; μέρη γαρ οίνον μιγνυντες, &c."

thus, in the Syriac Language, Echo has been happily styled "the Daughter of Voice."

That the kiss of a beloved mistress would add sweetness to the wine, is an idea very natural to a lover, and familiar to the poets. The second couplet of this Tetrastich may be nearly translated in the words of that well-known English Song.

"And when her lips the brim had prest,
"The cup with nectar flow'd."

The amorous Ovid wished to be the first to seize on the cup which his Mistress had just laid down, and would apply his lips to that part of it which her's had touched.

"*Quæ tu reddideris ego primus pocula sumam.*"
"*Et quâ tu biberis hac ego parte bibam*.*"

The jealous Queen of Heaven, as we read in Lucian, thus upbraided the inconstant Jove: "You drink from that "part of the cup, which my rival's lips have touched; so that "you blend a kiss with the nectar which you imbibe †."

And the reader will find in the Greek Romance of Achilles Tatius ‡, a charming description of the pleasure which Clito-

---

* Ovid, Amorum, Lib. i. Elegy 4.

† "Πίνεις, ὅθεν καί αὐτος ἔπιε, κ̀ ἔνθα προσέρμωσι τα χείλη, ἵνα κ̀ πίῃς ἅμα κ̀ φιλῇς."

‡ Ἐγὼ δὲ ἐπιτηρησας το μίσγω, &c.—See the loves of Clitophon and Leucippe, by Achilles Tatius—Book II.

phon

CHAP. VI.]   PERSIAN MISCELLANIES.   157

phon received from the kindnefs of his fair Leucippe, who repeatedly imprinted kiffes on the cup, which fhe knew her lover was to receive from the attendant Satyr*.

PLATE VIII. No. 5.

" *Beraumed bad-i feba va booee-i noorooz.*"

" The Weftern gale returns, and the fragrance of fpring."

IN this fpecimen, the letter *Sad*, of *Seba*, is joined to *Ba* by a long dafh, which only ferves to fill up the line, and perhaps, is confidered as ornamental. The point of *Ba*, is placed in the hollow of final *Hba*. The points of letters in this fpecimen, are of that fquare or diamond-like form, which I have beforementioned, in Chapter III.

THAT the rofe's fragrance, and the melody of the querulous nightingale, were among the Perfian poet's favourite themes, I

* " More amantuim," (fays a learned commentator) " qui fibi rebus ab amatis miffis, ofcula figere amant."—Pet. Moll's Notes on Daphn. and Chloe, 20.

have

have already, perhaps, too frequently remarked; I shall here, for the last time, mention them, and observe, that the refreshing western breeze, to which the flower lends its delightful odour, is found to be equally the subject of Persian poetry: being, with the Nightingale and Rose, the welcome harbinger of Spring.

To the luxurious Asiatic, the approach of that season is inconceivably grateful, which restores to him, the genial warmth of his native climate, with all those pleasures that follow in the train of Spring. The poets of every age and country, have delighted to sing the praises of the new year*. Anacreon, in a beautiful passage, describes the " Graces, as " furnishing themselves with roses, on its appearance†." Innumerable are the Persian odes and sonnets, in praise of this sweet season, which begin like that of Sàdi, (whom the present specimen is taken from,) and, which may be almost literally translated in the words of Petrarch‡.

" *Zefiro torna e l' bel tempo rimena.*"

* " There is, I believe," (says Doctor Johnson,) " scarce any poet of eminence, who " has not left some testimony of his fondness for the flowers, the zephyrs, and the warblers " of the Spring; nor has the most luxuriant imagination, been able to describe the sere- " nity, and happiness of the golden age, otherwise, than by giving a perpetual spring, as " the highest reward of uncorrupted innocence." *Rambler*, No. 5.

This learned writer, here alludes to the " *Ver erat æternum,*" of Ovid's Met. Lib. I. 3.

† Ἴδε ῥῶς ἴαρος φανέντος," &c. ODE 37.   ‡ Petrarch: Part I. Sonnet 269.

I MUST

CHAP. VI.]   PERSIAN MISCELLANIES.   159

I must here remark, that, in the manuscript, from which this specimen is extracted, the preposition *Ber*, was omitted by the original transcriber. But some critical reader having supplied it in the margin, I have followed his example, and adopted it, more especially, as it seems necessary to exactness of scansion.

PLATE VIII. No. 6.

" *Sawkya fuzli behaur too mubaruck bashud.*"
" Oh cup-bearer! may thy youth, sweet season of thy spring, be
" happy."

THE *Sin* in *Sawkya*, is a long waving flourish; the points of medial *Ya* are not exactly under that letter; the point of *Fa*, in *Fuzl*, appears rather belonging to the next letter; that of *Ba*, in *Behàr*, is placed under the *Ha*. In *Mubaruck*, the *Ba* is a little turned stroke; the upper limb of *Caf* does not join the perpendicular, and in the hook of *Caf*, is placed the *Ba*, of *Bashud*; the final *D*, in *Bashud*, is only an abrupt termination of the *Shin*. The line, in Persian orthography, is thus:

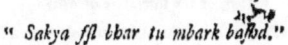

" *Sakya ffl bhar tu mbark bashd.*"

PERSIAN MISCELLANIES. [Chap. VI.

IN this specimen I have given the words of a Persian air, which, though in a style of melody by no means familiar to an European ear, possesses a considerable share of simplicity and sweetness. On the subject of music among the ancient Persians, which, with their painting, celebrated by *Nizami*, Sir William Jones believes to have perished irrecoverably*, I shall here be silent. The same learned Orientalist, is however, of opinion, that by a correct explanation of the best books on the Arabian and Persian systems of music, much of the old Greek theory may be recovered; and he believes, that the Persian system, like that of the Hindùs, has been formed on truer principles than our own; and that " all the skill of the native composers is directed to the great " object of their art, *the natural expression of strong passions*, " &c†."

I MUST here, however, remark, that the Arabians are said to be indebted for their knowledge of music to the more refined Persians; the variety and powers of their musical instruments are strongly and beautifully described in a short Poem of Hafiz, at the end of his Divaun, entitled the " Addrefs to the " Musician," or " *Mughenny Nameh*.‡" Chardin speaks

---

* Sir Wm. Jones's Anniversary Discourse on the Persians, 1789.
† Ibid, on the Literature of Asia, 1785.
‡ Of this Poem I shall speak more particularly in a future work.

scientifically

CHAP. VI.] PERSIAN MISCELLANIES. 161

scientifically of music, as cultivated by the Persians: M. Le Bruyn has described some of their instruments: twenty-two of which the excellent Kœmpfer has given engraved representations of; and the most learned Casiri, describing an ancient Arabic manuscript, informs us, that it contains a catalogue of musical instruments, to the number of thirty-one; for the most part, he says, originally Persian *.

THE origin of several instruments, and the history of the various modes of Persian music, are ingeniously treated of by Nakshebi, in his *Tooti-Nameh*, or " Tales of a Parrot†."

OF the Persian song given in the specimen, the musical notes were, with the words, communicated to me by an ingenious friend resident in the East: from him I received at the same time, the following little *Gazzel*, or *Love Song*, the

---

* See the Travels of Chardin and Le Bruyn. The plate given in Kœmpfer's Amœnitates Exoticæ, p. 741, and the Bibliotheca Arabico-Hispana, &c. of Casiri, Vol. i. 527.—See also, Herbelot, Bibl. Orient. Article "*Angam*."

† Of this very entertaining work, which contains fifty-two chapters, thirty-five of the tales have been abridged, and divested of their chief difficulties, by Mahommed Kadery, and printed with a literal English Version, opposite the Persian text, in one volume octavo, at Calcutta, 1792. In the same year also, a most excellent English translation of the first part of this work was published in London, by the Rev. Mr. Gerrans, in octavo. The beautiful imagery and flowery diction of the original, are judiciously retained in this translation, and it is to be hoped, that the learned gentleman will soon favour the public with a second volume.

Y

notes of which he committed to paper, from the voice of those singing girls of *Cashmere**, who wander from that delightful valley over the various parts of India; and I should have here gratified my musical readers with the original notes of both these Eastern compositions, but that my friend, whose exquisite skill, both practical and theoretic, qualifies him admirably for the task, has long been engaged in the study of oriental music, and has formed a large collection of Melodies, Persian, Hindù, and Cashmerian, which he will, probably, in a short time, offer to the public.

THE words of the Cashmerian Gazel, are these,

" *Ai dost, agur jaun tulbee,*
" *Jaun betoo bakhshem.*"

" Sweet Mistress! if you seek a Lover's heart and soul, behold I give
" thee mine!"

THESE simple words seem borrowed from a line beginning one of Sadi's Odes,

" *Gur jaun tulbee fuda-y-jaunet, &c.*"

---

* The province of Cashmere; where the Indians place their imaginary Paradise.— " Ejus modi beatitudinis locus, &c."—See Hyde's Relig. Vet. Pers. 173. Oxf. 1700; and the admirable account of this interesting country, in Major Rennels' Memoirs of the Map of Hindooftan, p. 132, &c.

AND

CHAP. VI.] PERSIAN MISCELLANIES. 163

AND here I cannot but obferve the extreme facility with which a Perfian lover gives up his heart, his foul, his life, to a beloved Miftrefs. He offers them for the earth on which fhe treads; and if fhe does not appear, his foul abandons his body. Thus in a valuable copy of the Divaun of *Senaï*, (a poet, whofe name is fcarcely known in Europe) the Lover declares, that " Life forfakes his frame when his beloved " is no longer near him; as the nightingale takes wing from " the garden, on the difappearance of the rofe."

" *Jaun rift az ten chun ber men yar niayed,*
" *Bulbul berud gul chu begulzar niayed.*"

THE Poet Jami fays, in one of the beautiful Sonnets that compofe his Divaun, " my inanimated body, it is true, con- " tinues here: but my foul accompanies the fair object of my " love, where'er fhe goes."

" *Beher menzil keh jaunaun men aunja-eft,*
" *Ten'em eenja vely jaun men aunja-eft.*"

AND Hafez, in the beginning of an admirable Ode, incul- cating perfeverance in amorous purfuits, declares " that he " will either refign his exiftence, or fucceed in the accom- " plifhment of his defires."

Y 2 " *Deft*

PERSIAN MISCELLANIES. [CHAP. VI.

" *Deft az tulb nedarem tu kam-i men berayed,*
" *Ya ten refed bejaunaun ya jaun az ten berayed.*"

THE exquifite play here, on the words *Jaun* and *Jaunaun*, to be fully comprehended only by a proficient in the Perfian, bids defiance to any adequate tranflation in our tongue. *Jaunaun*, a name which the lover not unfrequently beftows on the fair caufe of all his happinefs, is evidently derived from *Jaun*, the foul, life, &c. and correfponds with the ζωη και ψυχν, of the Greeks and the endearing terms " *vita mia, anima mia,*" of the Italians.

CHAPTER

CHAP. VII.] PERSIAN MISCELLANIES. 165

CHAPTER VII.

PLATE IX.

HUKAYUT *fee uhuſhtum*; *Nukkuleſt az Shaikh Aouz Sellameh Bagdady, (rahmet allah-alyeh) keh guft, Sheneed'um az walid khood keh wekta der keryet a Shaikh Metrbazray (rezy allah annaho) jeraud azeem, ecanny mellek buſiaur mikuzeſht: chendankeh temam puſheedeh ſhudeh buved. Va mekuddum iſhaun murdy buved firvvaur ber yek jeraud: ba'anvanz migoft. "La Illahilla allaho, Mohammed ruſool allahi, coll nimet femin allah." her janneh keh aun murd toocheh mi kurd mellek dumbal o miriſt: báad az aun, Shaikh Metrbazray der ſehn-e zawiet khood beroon aumed; va neda kurd; "Ya jenood allahi arjàa min huna!" der haul aun mellek heme baz keſhtend wa aun murd az huwa hemehu ikhauh peiſh ſhaikh auftad. Shaikh fermood aun murdra, " keh tera che baisſhud " keh begheer auzen bebeldet meu gedeſhty?"—aun murd der pay Shaikh auftad, umi booſed u azur mickhauſt, u iſtigſaur mikurd ta aunkeh Shaikh khoſhnud shud va aunche az o ſulub kurdeh buved baz dad; u fermud " berkheez u beròo," der haul aun murd baz der huwa pereed u rift hemehu teer, va aun mellek der belaud-e Iràk auftad va khulky aunra giriftend va kut khood mi ſaukhtend.*

ANECDOTE

ANECDOTE THE THIRTY EIGHTH,

(i. e. Of the Original Perfian Manufcript.)

IT is related of the Shaikh Aoufs Sellameh, of Bagdad, (the mercy of God be on him,) that he faid, "I have heard from my father, that once over the town, where Shaikh Meterbazray refided, (on whom be the peace of God,) there paffed an immenfe flight of locufts, fo numerous, that the whole country was nearly covered with them : and in the front of them, there was a man, riding upon a locuft, and he called out with a loud voice, " there is no God, " but God, and Mohammed is the prophet of God ; and is " not every bleffing from God ?" And to whatfoever fide that man directed his flight, the fwarm of locufts followed him. Then the Shaikh Meterbazray came forth into the court of his hermitage, and cried aloud, " O ye armies of the Lord, retire " from this place !" .inftantly the locufts retreated, and the man defcended from the air like an eagle, and fell at the feet of the Shaikh : and the Shaikh faid to the man, " wherefore haft " thou without permiffion, paffed over the place where I " refide ?" and the man fell at his feet and kiffed them, and repented, and intreated pardon, infomuch, that the Shaikh was appeafed, and all that the locufts had deftroyed, was reftored, .and the Shaikh faid, " arife and depart :" At that moment,

CHAP. VII.] PERSIAN MISCELLANIES. 167

the man darted into the air, with the fwiftnefs of an arrow, and the locufts defcended on the plains of Iràk, and the inhabitants thereof took them, and made them their food."

THE manufcript, from which this anecdote has been extracted, is written in a ftyle, neither very correct, nor elegant; but I thought it neceffary, that the reader fhould render himfelf acquainted with writing of that defcription, in which he will find but too many Oriental works tranfcribed. Before I proceed to analyze the graphical difficulties of this fpecimen, I fhall give the lines, containing exactly the words and letters of the original Perfian, arranged in their proper order; and, I would advife the reader, for his own convenience, and to facilitate his reference to the engraved fpecimen, to number the lines in the margin of the plate, fo that they may correfpond with the following:

1. Hhkayt fy u hfhtm .—Nklft az Shykh auzz Slamh Bgdady rhmt allh alyh——
2. kh gft fhnydm az wald khud kh wkty dr kryh Shykh Mtrbazray rfy allh. anh——
3. jrad azym yany mlkh bfyar mygzfht chndankh tmam pufhydhfhdh——
4. bud u mkdm ayfhan mrdy bud fuar br yk jrad b'auaz mygft laallh ala allh——

5. Mhhmd

168   PERSIAN MISCELLANIES.   [CHAP. VII.

5. Mhhmd rful allh kl namt fmn allh hr janb kh anmrd tuchh mykrd mlkh dnbal au——
6. myrft bad az an Shykh Mtrbazray dr fhn zauyh khud brun amd u nda
7. krd ya jnud allh arjay mn hna dr hal anmlkh hmh baz kfhtnd u an mrd az hua
8. hmchu akab pyfh Shykh aftad Shykh frmud anmrdra kh tra chh baas fhd kh bghyr
9. azn bbldh mn gdfhty an mrd drpay Shykh aftad u my bufyd u azr
10. mykhuaft u aftgfar mykrd taankh Shykh khfhnud fhd u anchh az u flb krdh
11. bud baz dad u frmud brkhyz u bru dr hal anmrd baz dr hua pryd u rft hmchu tyr
12. U an mlkh dr blad ark aftad u khlky anra grftnd u kut khud my fakhtnd.

WITH the affiftance of thefe printed lines, the reader, who has attended to the remarks in the fecond, third, and fourth Chapters, will find I hope, but few difficulties in the engraved fpecimen; thofe which remain for me to explain, appear to be the following words, in the

Firft line:—*Hufhtum*, written partly over the preceding *Sy* and *Waw*, and begun with a little turned *ha*; the ftroke of *Shin* in *Shaikh*, comes between that of *z* in *az*, and its point; in *Bagdady*, the point of *ba*, is placed under the firft *da*; in *Rehmet*, the points over final *ha*, (which make it *ta*,) are placed over the *Hha*; the fecond *Lam* in *Allah*, is very fhort, and in *Aleyeh*, above the line, no points are expreffed for *ya*.

Second line:—No points to *fa* and *ta*, in *Goft*; the *Alif* of *az*, touches the final *Mim*, of *Shencedehm*; in *Keryet*, the

ra

CHAP. VII.] PERSIAN MISCELLANIES. 169

ra hangs almoſt perpendicularly from the *Kaf;* in *Reſy,* the *ra* is a little oblique ſtroke, lying over the preceding letter; in the laſt word, *Annaho,* which is above the line, the point of *Nun* is placed over the long unmeaning daſh between that letter and final *ha.*

Third line:—IN *Jerad,* the *ra* is a continuation of the lower part of *Jim;* the initial *ya,* in *Eeauny,* is ſo long, as to appear like an *l;* the *Nun* is a turn of the pen, with a point over; *Melkh* is written ſo cloſe, and crowded, that the tail of *Kha,* touches that of the final *ya,* of *Eeauny,* the point of *Kha* is very high above it; under *Beſiaur* are placed three ſuperfluous points, for thoſe of *ba* and *ya* are not omitted; the point of *Zal,* in *Mikuzaſht,* almoſt touches that letter; in *Chendankeh,* the point of the ſecond *Nun* is ſeparated from its letter by the ſtroke of *Caf;* the points of *ta,* in *Temam,* almoſt touch the *Alif;* the ſtroke of *Shin,* touches the initial *pa,* in *Puſheedeh;* *pa* has but one point. *Shudeh* above the line.

Fourth line:—In *Iſhaun,* the points of *Shin* are irregularly placed; no points to final *ya* in *Murdy,* nor to that letter, when final, throughout the ſpecimen; the point of *ba,* in *Buzed,* under the *Waw;* over the words *Ba' avauz,* is placed the orthographical mark, *Medda;* as the *Alif* of *ba* is ſuppreſſed, and the letter *b* joined at once to the *Alif* of *Avauz,* it ſhould be *Ba avauz;* for the *z* of this word, no point is expreſſed; in *Migoſt,* the points of *ya* are thrown under the *ſa,* which is

Z   crowded

crowded into the hollow of *Gaf*; the three laſt letters of *Allah* are above the line.

Fifth line:—Over the word *Allah*, which occurs twice in this line, is placed the mark *Teſhdid*; the *ta*, in *Nimet*, expreſſed by final *ha*, with points; in *Semen*, the tail of *Nun* touches the point: the *h*, in *Her*, appears like an initial *Mim*: the words *Aun* and *Murd* are joined; the *Nun*, which ſhould be final, being placed before the *Mim*, as initial. (See p. 61. and 62:)

Sixth line:—In the word *Mirift*, a little ſtroke is negligently brought from the end of final *ta*, and touches the points. *Shaikh* is thrown over the words *az aun*, and *Sehn* over the preceding *dr*; the *za* of *Zawiyet* is placed over the final *Nun* of *Sehn*; the point of *Kha*, in *Khud*, is over the *Waw*, and that of *Nun*, in the laſt word *Neda*, is rather over the preceding copulative *Waw*.

Seventh line:—In *Jenud* the points of *Jim* and *Nun* are not regularly placed: in *Arjaa*, the firſt ſyllable comes between the letter *Jim* and its point: a blot in *Min*: a long turned ſtroke between the *n* and *Alif* of *Hena*: in *Kuſhtend* the points of *ta* and *Nun* are blended together; and the letter *ha*, of *Huwa*, comes between the points of *za*, in *az*, and its letter.

Eighth line:—In *Hemchu* one point for three in *Chim*; the tail of final *ba*, in *Ykab*, touches the *pa* in *Peiſh*, which is deſcribed without any points for *Shin*; the *Dal*, of *Aftad*, in the hollow

CHAP. VII.]   PERSIAN MISCELLANIES.   171

hollow of *Shaikh*; the point of *Nun*, in *Aunmurdra*, is over the *Mim*; the points of *Sa*, in *bais*, confused; that of *Ghain*, in *Begheer*, not exactly over its proper letter.

Ninth line: THE points of the two *bas*, in *Bebcldeh*, are joined; *men* badly expressed; the points of *ta*, in *Aftad*, are placed over the *Alif*; and under the word *boofeed*, are three superfluous points. (See page 52.)

Tenth line:—THE *Waw*, after *Mikhauft*, so described as to seem belonging to the following word, *Iftigfaùr*, of which the initial *Alif* is under the stroke of *Sin*; and three superfluous points are also placed under this word; in *Aunkeh* the stroke of *Caf* is between *Nun* and its point; the points of *Kha, Shin*, and *Nun*, in *Khofhnud*, are confusedly thrown together, one point for *Chim* in *Auncheh*, and no upright body for *Nun*.

Eleventh line:—IN the word *Kheez*, the points of *Kha* and *Zu* are united; the *Waw*, after *Pereed*, appears like a *Dal*, and seems to belong to the next word *Rift*; *Hemchu* is almost perpendicular; one point for *Chim*: the *ya*, in *Teer*, a slight turn of the pen.

Twelfth line:—THE point of *N*, in *Aun*, touches the letter; that of *Ba*, in *Belad*, not under its proper letter; the *Ra*, of *Irak*, comes suddenly from the *Ain*, the *Kaf* very much hooked: in *Khulky* the points of *Kaf* almost touch the *Lam*; the points of *Ta*, and *Nun*, in *Griftend*, blended; as are those of the last word *Saukhtend*, of which the *Alif* is not straight.

Z 2   THERE

THERE is not, I believe, any combination of letters, or instance of irregularity in this specimen, which may not be found minutely analyzed in the former chapters of this work, to which the reader must often turn, if he wishes to render himself master of coarsely written Talik.

WHEN I assure the reader that this specimen of miraculous anecdotes has not been extracted from the original collection, as possessing a greater share of absurdity than the others, he will endeavour to persuade himself with me, for the honour of mankind, that the credulity of extreme ignorance alone, could, in any age or country, have been amused by such idle fictions; and he will lament, that superstition, or a knavish desire of imposing on the multitude, could induce any person, particularly a writer of eminence, to mis-spend his time in the compilation, and I may say, the composition, of such tales.

YET we find, that in works of this nature, *Yafëi al Yemini*, a celebrated Arabian author, employed his pen, and has left voluminous records, of the miracles performed by his compatriot saints. Of one among these, surnamed *Shaikh Abdelcader*,

CHAP. VII.]   PERSIAN MISCELLANIES.   173

*Abdélcader**, he has written the life in a diſtinct volume; but of many others, inferior perhaps in piety, or wonder-working powers, he has given a confiderable number of anecdotes, collected in the work called " *Roud'a'r'yaheen*," or the " Garden " of odoriferous Herbs;" from a tranſlation of this work, into the Perſian language, I have extracted the ſpecimen here given.

THIS Perſian tranſlation contains two hundred ſections; in each, one anecdote, but in ſome, two or three ſhort ſtories of the ſame ſaint are related under one head; and in many, are given lines of Arabic poetry, always on moral or religious ſubjects, of which there is not any tranſlation. In favour of the ſtyle and language of this work, I can ſay but little: a ſuperficial knowledge of Perſian will enable the reader to perceive that the tranſlator, long habituated probably to the peruſal of Arabic writings, has negligently adopted words and idioms from that tongue, which thoſe of the Perſian would have expreſſed as well.

* The word Shaikh, ſignifies not only an ancient, and venerable perſonage, as in the ſpecimen; but often means the head, or chief man, of a tribe or family. The ſcrupulous piety of the Mahometans will not permit the names of any ſaint, or holy elder, to be written or uttered, without the benediction ſuitable to his rank, or degree of ſanctity, although the name were to occur frequently in the ſame page or diſcourſe; two inſtances of theſe benedictions are given in the ſpecimen.

BUT

But many of thefe anecdotes prefent curious and original pictures of the domeftic life and manners of the Arabs: and could they be divefted of the difgufting fuperftition, which prevails through all, would furnifh, in a tranflation, fome ufeful hints on the geography, cuftoms, and natural hiftory of Arabia.

On the fubject of the miracle, recorded in the anecdote before us, I fhall offer a few obfervations; though fortunately for the inhabitants of thefe northern climates, the natural hiftory of the locuft, is to them, a matter of fmall concern; but the havoc and defolation which attend this winged peft, wherefoever it directs its flight, feem to juftify the Arabian faint, in addreffing them, as the " forces of the Lord," for, like a numerous and well ordered army, commiffioned by offended heaven, to inflict famine and its horrors on fome devoted land, thefe deftructive animals defcend, as it were, from the clouds, and lighting on the green fields, devour all the tender plants and growing herbage, and render vain the labours of the hufbandman.

Father Angelo mentions the clouds of locufts, eclipfing the fun, which pafs from Arabia into Perfia; the alarm of the inhabitants, and the means they ufe to prevent the lighting of thofe deftructive animals on their fields; he alfo defcribes the fmall birds which devour them with incredible expedition

and

CHAP. VII.]   PERSIAN MISCELLANIES.

and avidity, and the equal degree of "*Gusto*," with which the Arabians eat a dish of locusts boiled in water and salt.*

From the order and regularity of their flight, the confused buzzing and noise occasioned by their wings, the terror they inspire, and other circumstances, we find, that by the most ancient writers, locusts have been compared to a powerful army, going forth to battle, with the tumult of chariots, and war horses. In a most learned and elaborate essay, the celebrated Bochart has quoted various parts of Scripture, in which they

* Gazoph. Persicum, Art. Locusta, 201 202, "*In Arabia tutti quanti mangiavo queste locuste con sommo gusto, &c.*" The following extract from a very respectable traveller will serve to express the desolation and misery attendant on those unwelcome visitants. "Les " habitans de la campagne et des villes d'alentour avoient etè ruineè par des sauterelles, " qui etoient venües fondre sur leurs terres, apres avoir mangè toutes les semailles de la " Judea et de la Palestine : elles avoient devorè les bleds, les cotons, et toutes leurs " denrees, et affamè cette province a un point que, n'aiant rien pû recueillir l'anneè prece- " dente, ces pauvres paisans n'etoint plus en ètat de paier au Beig ce qu'ils devoient tous " les ans au Grand Seigneur." A serious revolt was the natural consequence of the in- solvency of those unfortunate peasants, as the Beig, or Viceroy above-mentioned, en- deavoured to enforce the payment of the usual tribute to the Grand Signior.—See the " Voyage au Camp du Grand Emir :"—" par le Chevalier D'Arvieux," p. 91. Oct. Paris, 1717.

This work has appeared in English, and a most excellent translation of it into the Dutch language, with learned and ingenious notes; was published at Utrecht, in one vol. octavo, 1780, by the Rev. G Kuipers, Preacher of Dort, in Holland, under the title of "*Reis* " *naar den Grooten Emir.*"

are

are so described, particularly the books of Joel, Amos, Job, &c.* But the authority of the Arabian Shaikh for styling them, as in the anecdote before us, "the armies of the Lord," seems to be the following tradition, handed down by Mahometan authors†. Their prophet, say they, forbade that locusts should be killed; for one of them falling on a certain time into his hands, he found written on the creature's wings, "*Nehen jenud allah al'akber, &c.*" "We are the army of the "mighty God: we have each ninety and nine eggs, and had we "but the hundredth we would consume the world, and all that "it contains." We find, however, that notwithstanding the prohibition of the Arabian Prophet, the inhabitants of *Irâk,* (the ancient Chaldea) like the Hebrews of old,‡ and St John in the wilderness of Judea,§ used these animals as food; and I believe the custom of eating them prevails all over Africa and Asia. Leo Africanus, after describing the immense swarms of locusts that infested Barbary, intercepting the very sun-beams, adds, that they are not esteemed by the people of Lybia and Arabia Deserta as a bad omen; for they dry them in the sun, pulverise, and eat them.‖

* Hierozoicon: Chap. iv. book iv.
† Al-Damir, Ebn'Omar, &c.—See Bochart's Hierozoicon, b. iv. chap. iv.
‡ Leviticus.   § St. Matthew.
‖ Leo Africanus, Book ix; a dish of locusts, so prepared, is called in Arabic "*cochijei;*" they are eaten plain, or mixed with fat.—See Richardson's Dictionary, vol. 1. 2075.

CHAP. VII.] PERSIAN MISCELLANIES. 177

OF the two hundred anecdotes contained in the original work of *Yafeï al Yemini*, many seem to have been borrowed from the traditions of other countries. Several of the Arabian Saints restored sight to the blind, hearing to the deaf; nay, some had the power of raising from the dead. But I shall forbear to draw any invidious parallel between our Mahometan miracles, and those legends which amused the bigotted and superstitious, in the ages of European darkness; nor shall I ope the ponderous volume in which these are recorded, and which lies covered with the dust of oblivion, even on the monastic shelf. It is to be hoped, that such fictions can no longer amuse the credulity of mankind: and that the Arab of the present day, whose belief is the Creed of pure Theism*, (when divested of its absurd conclusion,†) can find but little pleasure in the perusal of those tales, which ascribe to mortals the possession of such power as can be the attribute of GOD alone.

* " *La Allah illa Allah!*" There is no GOD but GOD!

† " *Waw Muhammud Rifiul Allah*;" and Mahomet is the Prophet of GOD.

A a   CHAP-

CHAPTER VII.

FRONTISPIECE.

" *Biya ay yſhk, por afsoon va neerunk,*
" *Keh baſhud kuritoo keh fuluh va keh jung.*

" *Gahy furzaneh ra diwàneh fazee,*
" *Gahy diwàneh ra furzauneh fazee.*

" *Chu ber zulf-i peri-rooyaun nehy bund,*
" *Bezunjeer-a junoon auftad khruydmund:*

" *Wa gur az aun zulf bundy berkuſhaeey,*
" *Cheraugi-akl yabed ruſhenaÿ.*

" *Zeleekha yekſbeby beefabr va beehooſh,*
" *Beghumm hemzad u ba mehennet hem ageoſt,*

" *Zejaum-i derd, durd aſhaumeey kurd,*
" *Zefooz-i yſhk bee araumeey kerd.*"

" Come,

" Come, oh Love, with all your fafcinations and deceitful charms; you who are
" the promoter of concord and of ftrife.

" At one time you make the wife man filly; and at another time you infpire
" wifdom into the fool.

" When you place your fnare in the ringlets of beautiful damfels, the wifeft
" man falls into the fetters of infanity:

" But if you fhould loofe this fnare from the fair one's ringlets, the lamp of rea-
" fon will refume its light.

" Zeleekha, one night, impatient and diftracted: the twin-fifter of affliction,
" and to whom forrow was as a familiar friend,

" Drank to the very dregs of the cup of wretchednefs, and from the burning
" anguifh of paffion paffed the night without repofe."

AS I gave in the laft fpecimen a page of profe, rather coarfely written, I fhall conclude this work by prefenting to the reader, fix couplets of Perfian Poetry, from a manufcript, of which the writing is correct, and the combinations of letters formed with fome degree of elegance. The original order is as follows:

I.

1. Bya ay afhk pr afsun u nyrnk
2. Kh bafhd kar tu kh fhh u kh jnk.

II.

II.

3. Ghy frzanhra dyuanh fazy
4. Ghy dyuanhra frzanh fazy.

III.

5. Chu br zlf pry ruyan nhy bnd
6. Bznjyr jnun aftad khrdmnd.

IV.

7. U gr zan zlf bndy brkſhayy
8. Chragh akl yabd ruſhnayy.

V.

9. Zlykha ykſhby byſbr u byhuſh
10. Bghm hmzad u ba mhhnt hmaghuſh.

VI.

11. Z jam drd *drd* aſhamyy krd
12. Zſuz aſhk by aramyy krd.

THAT the reference from this fcheme to the plate may be more eafy to the reader, I have numbered every couplet, and diſtinctly, the lines of each couplet; and, I think he will find it uſeful to mark, in like manner, the Roman figures with his pencil, in the margin of the plate. I ſhall not be very minute in my obſervations on this ſpecimen, as I ſuppoſe the ſtudent to be, by this time, pretty nearly maſter of the chief difficulties

of

CHAP. VII.]   PERSIAN MISCELLANIES.   181

of the Talik hand; and as I am befides of opinion, that it will be for his advantage, to decipher the lines before him, by means of the printed fcheme juft given, and frequent reference to the former chapters of this work; it being certain that, that knowledge, which is the refult of our own labours, and diligent inquiry, finks deeper into the memory, than that which we carelefsly borrow from another.

I shall only remark, that the points of *ba* and *ya*, are generally blended, as in *Biya*, (the 1ft line) and in *Beefabr* and *Beeboofh*, (9th line); alfo thofe of *jim* and *ya* in the word *Zunjeer*, (6th line); a long dafh unites two letters in fome words, as in *Furzauneh*, (3d and 4th lines) and in *Akl*, (8th line) in which word, the points of *Kaf* are placed over the dafh, and the hook of *Lam* touches the *ya* of the next word *Yabed*; the point of *jim* in *Junk*, (2d line) is placed under the *Gaf*; and in the words *Deewaneh Safy* of the (3d line), the point of *za* is placed over the *Sin*; in the hollow of final *nun*, in *Rooceaun* (5th line) is placed the final *ya* of *Nehy*; and in *Bezunjeer*, (6th line) the point of *nun* is over the *ra*; the points of fome letters are placed perpendicularly one over the other, as in *Yfhk*, (1ft line) and *Kufhayy*, (7th line); the word *Derd* is diftinguifhed from *Durd*, in the 11th line, by the *Fatha* over it, the latter having *Damma*; fee Chapter IV. p. 68. A catch-word *(Kefhud,)* leads to the next page, as I before obferved, Chapter IV.

In

> In amore hæc omnia infunt vitia,
> Sufpiciones, inimicitiæ, induciæ, injuriæ
> Bellum pax rurfum.
>
> TERENT. Eun. I. 1.

FOR the fpecimen of Perfian writing, which is to conclude this work, I have chofen the beginning of a Chapter, in the celebrated poem, "*Eufef ve Zeleekha**," of which the title has been already given in Plate V. No. 5.

THE loves of the Hebrew Patriarch, Jofeph, with the fair Zeleekha, who, in the Old Teftament, is called the wife of Potiphar, and by fome Arabian hiftorians, Raïl†, are the fubject of this poem. The author, whofe name is Jamî‡, a writer

---

* So are thefe names pronounced, as I have been affured in the letter of an ingenious correfpondent from the Eaft ; but they have been written in various ways by many learned Orientalifts ; Eufoof, Jufuf, Zulikha, Zoleikha, &c.

† See Notes to Sale's Koran, Chapter Jofeph; befides the original Quarto, and that in two volumes Octavo ; of this valuable work, a new edition has appeared this year, (1795) at Bath, in Octavo, two volumes. Neither does the Old Teftament, nor the Koran, mention the name of Jofeph's miftrefs; but all the later Afiatic writers agree, in calling her Zeleekha.

‡ See an account of Jamî, page 17, &c.

CHAP. VII.]   PERSIAN MISCELLANIES.   183

of the firft clafs, has decorated, with all the graces of poetry, the romantic ftory of the youthful Canaanite, as related in the Koran*, where indeed, we find it ftrangely altered from the original Mofaic narrative; but the charms of the Egyptian lady, which the poet celebrates, as well as her name, are neither recorded in the Old Teftament†, nor fpoken of by Mohammed : her paffion, however, for Jofeph, and her beauty, are the fubject of many poems, ranked among the fineft compofitions in the languages of Afia. A Turkifh writer‡, declares that,

" *Temam mefridehi Zeleekhaden koozuk khatoon yughidy.*"

" In all Egypt, there was no woman more beautiful than " Zaleekha;" and the charms of Jofeph, the Adonis of the Eaft, are become proverbial, and alluded to by all the Lyrick poets

---

* In fupport of a favourite fyftem, the moft learned men often adduce extraordinary arguments : a very ingenious writer has drawn a clofe parallel between our Jofeph of the Scriptures, and the Proteus of prophane hiftory, in a work, profeffedly written to prove, that Herodotus, while defcribing the affairs of Egypt, was the inconfcious hiftorian of the Jewifh people. See *Herodote Hiftorien du peuple Hebreu fans le favoir*," Second Edition, Liege, 1790, p. 23, Octavo. This work, however, is only a defence of the " *Hiftoire Veritable des Tems Fabuleux*," by the Abbé Guerin du Rocher, in 3 vols.

† Genefis, xxxix, &c.

‡ Quoted in " Seaman's Turkifh Grammar, p. 22, Quarto, Oxford, 1670.

in their gazels or sonnets, as well as by those who have made his story the subject of longer and more regular poems; thus *Hafez* in a charming ode, addressing some beautiful youth, declares, that " all the world pronounced him the Joseph of " the age," a second Adonis;

" *Goftend khulayek keh too-cey Eusoof sany.*"

AND, in another ode, he styles him the " Moon of " Canaan."

" *Mah-i Canaani men musnedy Mesr ani too shud,*
" *Gah i aunest keh pedrüdi kuni zendaunra.*"

" O my moon of Canaan! the throne of Egypt is thine own,
" This is the time that thou shouldst bid farewell to prison*."

THE

---

* The first line of this couplet is given in the Persian Grammar, by Sir Wm Jones; I have here, for the last time, quoted the name of him whose writings induced me to deviate from the beaten paths of classic learning, and to wander among the flowery fields of Asiatic literature: A name already so celebrated by happier pens than mine, that it is unnecessary to enumerate in this place the various original compositions in Latin, English, and French, of the voluminous Jones: his admirable translations from the Arabian, Persian, and Sanscrit languages, his learned writings as a Lawyer, and his elegant productions as a Poet. The universality of his genius is acknowledged by many contemporary writers, and so great was his stock of acquired knowledge, that the name of Sir William Jones, is sufficient to express the highest degree of intellectual excellence that a human being could attain.

CHAP. VII.]   PERSIAN MISCELLANIES.   185

THE imprisonment of Joseph, here alluded to by Hafez, affords subject for some very interesting chapters of that poem of Jaumi, from which the specimen is extracted; the enamoured Zelcekha is there supposed to declare, that

" *Chu zendaun jauy-i insaun Gul azaur est,*
" *Neh zendaun, bel keh khurmi nubuhaur est.*"

" WHEN a prison becomes the residence of such a lovely rose-cheeked mor-
" tal, it loses all the horrors of a prison, and possesses all the charms of spring.".
" But,"

Adds she in another place,

attain. His eulogium, and his elegy, have lately fallen from the pens of Hayley the poet, and Maurice, the learned author of the " Indian Antiquities." But the brevity and singular beauty of the Epitaph, written by a brother judge (Sir Wm. Dunkin), induce me to present it to the reader as the best conclusion of this note :

Gulielmus Jones eques : Cur. sup. in Bengal ex judicibus unus;
Legum peritus, fidusque interpres :
Omnibus benignus,
Nullius fautor :
Virtute, fortitudine, suavitate morum
Nemini Secundus :
Seculi eruditi longè primus,
Ibat ubi solum plura cognoscere Fas est.
27 April, 1794.

B b   " If

"If in paradife we were not to behold the face of the perfon we adore,
"paradife itfelf would appear dreary to a longing lover's eye."

"*Bulu bee rooee y jaunaun gur behisht-eft,*
"*Bcheshim-i aushek-i mushtak zusht-eft.*"

On the fubject of the former couplet, I fhall remark, that the idea of a dungeon or any other difagreeable place, made delightful when inhabited by the object of one's love, feems fo natural to thofe really affected by that paffion, that I believe it will be found in the poetry of every age and nation; few have fo fweetly expreffed a thought of this nature, as the amorous Tibullus,

"Sic ego fecretis poffum bene vivere fylvis,
"Quà nulla humano fit via trita pede,
"Tu mihi curarum requies, tu nocte vel atrà,
"Lumen, et in folis tu mihi turba locis*."

This beautiful paffage has Hammond, the gentle difciple of the Latin Poet, thus happily paraphrafed; though perhaps no verfion into another tongue can do juftice to the *Curarum requies* and the *turba* of the original.

* Tibull: Eleg. 13:—Ad Amicam, Lib. iv.

"With

CHAP. VII.] PERSIAN MISCELLANIES.

> " With thee in gloomy defarts let me dwell,
> " Where never human footftep mark'd the ground,
> " Thou light of life! all darknefs can't expel,
> " And feem a world with folitude around."

On the fubject of the laft quoted Perfian couplet of Jaumi, I muft again introduce Tibullus, who has beautifully anticipated the idea of a Mahometan paradife; of which I believe the black-eyed Houries conftitute the principal felicity. The Poet and the Prophet are alike rewarded with the fmiles of beauty; a celeftial virgin receives into her bofom, the ardent Afiatic, and Venus herfelf conducts the amorous Roman into the Elyfian bowers.

> " Sed me, quod facilis tenero fum femper amori,
> " Ipfa Venus campos ducet in Elyfios*."

To return to the hiftory of Jofeph, I fhall mention one, among the various poems and romances that have been founded on it: a work, in the Englifh language, which, as well as its author, is but little known, I mean the curious poem, " Egypt's Favorite," by Sir Francis Hubert, Knt. (printed in Duod. London, 1631.) It follows one, in the copy before me, by

---

* Tibull. Lib. 1. Eleg. 3. ad miffalam.

the fame author, intitled, "The Hiftoric of Edward the "Second, furnamed Carnarvon, one of our Englifh kings, "together with the fatall down-fall," &c. &c. printed in 1629. This is not the place to prefent the reader with an extract from the latter work, which is ingenious and interefting. But the poem of "Egypt's Favorite," is divided into four parts, viz:

"Jofephus in Puteo ;—or, The Unfortunate Brother,
"Jofephus in Gremio ;—or, The Chafte Courtier,
"Jofephus in Carcere ;—or, The Innocent Prifoner,
"Jofephus in Summo ;—or, The Noble Favorite ;
"Together with Old Ifrael's progrefs into the Land of
"Gofhen."

As a fpecimen of this extraordinary poem, I fhall give a few lines from the fecond part, in which Jofeph begins the account of his misfortunes, and the original caufe of his imprifonment, alluded to in the Perfian couplets before quoted :

XV.
"My lady-miftreffe caft an amorous eye
"Upon my forme, which her affections drew :
"Shee was Love's martyr, and in flames did frye,
"But (like a woman) did that love purfue,

XVI.
"Wifely and cunningly, &c. &c.

AND

CHAP. VII.]   PERSIAN MISCELLANIES.   189

AND he thus begins the third part of his ſtory :

" From hopes of court to horrors of a jayle,
" From great reſpect, from friends, from wealth, from place :
" Unto a loathſome dungeon without bayle,
" A woſull fall—yet this was Joſeph's caſe." &c.

BUT I ſhall conclude my obſervations on the Hiſtory of the Hebrew Patriarch, and cloſe this volume, by remarking, that the Perſian Romance, has altered many circumſtances, even from the Koran ; and that the cataſtrophe, in particular, of the heroine's amorous ſchemes, ſo diſgraceful, according to the records of Moſes, and of Mohammed, is deſcribed by the poet Jamì, as crowning her paſſion with ſucceſs, and uniting her in marriage with the object of her love.

SUCH

SUCH are the obfervations on Perfian manufcripts, which I promifed to the reader, in the beginning of this work, with my own remarks, and the quotations from other writers, which I have profufely fcattered through it, in the form of fhort and diftinct effays, hoping thereby, to relieve the reader, and diverfify, in fome meafure, the barren famenefs of my original fubject. The number of examples might have been augmented, and this volume fwelled to a much greater bulk, by fpecimens of highly ornamented manufcripts; but neither have I had leifure for adding more, nor do fuch additions feem neceffary; for as I have already obferved, the principles of Perfian writing are exactly the fame, whether the letters be formed with elegance and tafte, or fcrawled with inaccuracy and difregard of beauty.

Such as it is, I prefent this Effay to the public; but too confcious of its manifold defects, and of my own inability, from want of time to render it more correct; let the indulgent reader receive it as a work, begun without any intention of publication, irregularly continued amid the duties and diffipations of a military life, and now, abruptly concluded, on the eve of embarkation for an hoftile fhore: I offer it, with the hope alone, that it may prove ufeful, till fome other perfon fhall have improved on my plan, or framed a better.

CHAP. VII.]   PERSIAN MISCELLANIES.

AFTER all, a few weeks ſtudy of good authors, and frequent tranſcribing from correct originals, will render this work, or any other of the ſame kind, unneceſſary; but the induſtry of others, and our own wiſhes, will be vain, without application and perſeverance.

CHESTER,
March 27, 1794.

LONDON,
September, 1795.

SINCE my return from the Continent, I have been induced to make ſome alterations, and to inſert a few quotations from books, printed during the preſent year, in the original manuſcript, which was cloſed, as the reader may have perceived, early in the laſt. Before I finally diſmiſs it, I ſhall mention another circumſtance in the hiſtory of this work, becauſe, while it points out the chief ſource of its faults, it may ſerve, perhaps, as an extenuation of them; it is, that, until offered to the world in its preſent form, this Eſſay has not fallen under the inſpection of any human eye but that of the author.

HAD

Had I solicited the assistance of those among my friends, who were celebrated for eloquence, or distinguished by profundity of learning, this work, might now, perhaps, boast of diction more refined, and be enriched with fragments of classical erudition. But, when I considered, that, within the circle of my acquaintance, Oriental Literature had been but little cultivated, and the languages of Asia almost totally unknown, I became apprehensive that sufficient attention might not be paid to the general design of my work, and that its chief object might be altogether forgotten, while one would reduce, and another add; some advise total rejection of passages, and some suggest partial alteration. I therefore early resolved to charge myself alone with the burden of responsibility for all its faults; and, as I shall submit, without a murmur, to the correcting lash of criticism, nor attempt to throw it from myself on others, so I indulge the hope of possessing, undivided, whatever recompense of approbation the public shall bestow on one who has honestly endeavoured to please, and to instruct.

A VOCABU-

A
VOCABULARY

OF THE

ARABIC AND PERSIAN WORDS

WHICH OCCUR IN THIS WORK.

A.

Afak, universe, quarters of the world
Afrasiaub, a proper name
Afsoon, charms, fascination
Aftaub, the sun
Agleb, superior, most part
Agoosh, embrace, the bosom
Agur, or *Gur*, if
Aherimaun, the Devil
Aimun, free, exempt
Ai, or *Ay*, Oh! Ho!
Ajz, weak, imbecillity
Akber, most great, powerful
Akl, reason, sense
Akser, in general, most part
Al, Arab. article, "the"
Aley-hi, to, or, upon him
Allah, GOD
Am, I am
Amber, ambergris, amber,
And, they are
Andisheh, thoughts, anxiety
Anduh, grief, trouble, &c.
Ankaboot, spider
Annaho, on him, to him
Ar, for *Agur*, if
Araumy, rest, repose
Arjad, retire, *Arab. Imper.*
Arzoo, desire, wish
Ashaumeey, a draught
Ashk, a tear
Ashufteh, enamoured, perplexed
Asp, a horse

VOCABULARY.

Ej, or *Eft*, he is, it is
Iab, water
Audmy, a human creature, a man
Auftadeh-deu, fallen, to fall
Aumedeft, from
Aumêdun, to come
Aumeez, partic. of
Aumeekhtun, to mix
Aumeed'um, my hope
Aun, that
Aunchê, that which
Aunchunaun, thus, fo, &c.
Aunkeh, he, or fhe who,
Aunja, there, in that place
Aunra, oblique cafe of *Aun*.
Aufhek, a lover
Autifh, fire
Auvauz, a clamour, noife
Aurvurd, he brought, from *Aurwurden*, to bring
Auzen, leave, permiffion
Awlad, children, race, &c.
Az, from, of, than
Azem, and *Azeem*, great, large
Azur, forgivenefs, pardon.

B.

Ba, with
Baad, after, afterwards
Baad az aun, after that, then
Bad, let it be, *Mebad*, let there be not

Bad, the wind, *Bade-e Suba*, the Zephyr
Bagdady, a perfon of Bagdad
Baïs, occafion, caufe
Bakfhem, I would give
Bala, above, upon
Balkh, the capital of Choraffan
Bar, a load, a time, turn, &c.
Bafhud, he, or it may be
Bafhy, you may be
Baug, a garden
Baz, again
Bazy, or *Bauzy*, play, fport
Bebeldet, comp. of *b*, in, to, on, and
Beldet, a town, village, &c.
Bee, without
Beened, he fees
Beeny, you fee, obferve
Beeroon, out, out of
Befatha, with the mark *Fatha*
Begheer, without
Behaur, or *Buhaur*, the fpring
Beher, to, or in all, every
Beheter, better
Behifht, Paradife
Beiya, come, ho! bring thou
Bekurd, is made, rendered
Belaud, towns, diftricts
Bemen, to me
Belkeh, but, however, but if
Bemaued, remains, let remain
Ber, on, upon, the bofom

VOCABULARY.

Beray, for, on account of
Berayud, arifes, goes, fucceed, &c.
Bergirift, took up, &c.
Berift, went, departed
Berkheez, arife thou
Berkuſhay, you open, loofe
Beroo, go, go away
Berud, goes away
Befiaur, much, many, &c.
Befteh, bound, clofed
Betoo, to, in, or with you
Beyekbar, at one time, at once
Bezungeer, in, or to the chain
Bikeraun, infinite, ineftimable
Bikyas, without bounds
Biroon, out, out of
Biya, come! bring, &c.
Bokhará, a city
Booce, fmell, perfume
Boomy, the owl
Boofédun, to kifs
Boofeh, a kifs
Buee, or *Booe*, fmell, &c.
Buhaur, or *Behaur*, fpring
Bulbul, the Perfian Nightingale
Bulee, yes, but, however
Bund, a fetter, fnare, bonds, &c.
Burden, to bear, carry
Burf, fnow
Burved, or *Bood*, he was, it was
Buzruk, great, large

C.

Caf, a fabulous mountain
Canaàn, Paleftine
Chè, or *Cheh*, who, what, wherefore, why, whom, &c.
Chehar, four
Chehel-Minar, the forty pillars, or the ruins of ancient Perfepolis
Chehreh, face, air, mien, &c.
Chekur, the heart, liver, &c.
Chenaun, fo, fuch, &c.
Chenauncheh, thus, in the fame way
Chendanukeh, as many as, more as, &c.
Cheraugh, lamp, torch, candle,&c.
Cherekh, fphere, circle, &c.
Cheſhim, the eye
Cheſhimhay, pl. the eyes
Chu, as like, when
Chun, when, fince, as, like, &c.

D.

Dad, equity, he gives, a gift
Dameu, a fold, hem, fkirt
Daniſtun, to know
Dara, Darius, King of Perfia
Daree-ud, you have, they have
Daſhtun, to have, hold
Daughy, a fear, wound, mark
Dehanuy, the mouth
Deed, he faw
Deeden, to fee

VOCABULARY.

Deedeh, particip. seen, eye
Deeve, a Dæmon, Evil Spirit
Deewauneh, insane, mad, foolish
Der, in, upon, into, &c.
Derd, affliction, grief
Derïay, waves, sea
Derung, delay, hesitation
Dest, the hand
Digur, other, else
Dil, the heart
Dilaraumy, rest of the heart
Dildar, possessing the heart, a mistress
Dilfereeb, deceiving the heart
Dilruba, ravishing the heart
Diraz, long
Doo, or *Du*, two
Door, or *Dur*, far
Dost, the hand, a friend, mistress
Dosteh, handful, a nosegay
Duhur, fortune
Dumbal, tail, track, vestige, rere
Dur, far
Durd, dregs, sediment
Dureegh, alas!
Durusty, truth, sincerity
Duset, a mistress, a friend.
Dyar, houses, mansions

E.

Eaunèe, that is to say, viz.
Een, or *aèn*, this, *Eenja*, here

Endam, form, stature, &c.
Endisheh, see *Andisheh*
Esh, *his*, or *hers*, added to nouns, as *Jemaul-esh*, his beauty
Est, or *ast*, he, she, or it is.

F.

Fatha, an orthographical mark
Femin, but from, &c. Arab. comp. of the particle of and *min*, from, &c.
Ferda, to-morrow
Fereeb, deceiving
Ferghend, ivy
Feringy, European
Ferish, a bed, couch, cushion
Ferishtèh, an angel, messenger
Feyset, grace, plenty
Fermuden, or *Firmuden*, to command, to say, &c.
Fi, in
Firaukh, abundant, large, &c.
Firzendeh, a son, child, offspring
Foru, or *Foru*, down, below, &c.
Fuday, a ransom, price
Furzauneh, wife, learned, &c.
Fust, *Fust-i behaur*, spring, season
Futtah, victory.

G.

Gahy, time, at one time, opportunity

VOCABULARY.

Geety, the world
Gercheh, although
Geshty, a ship, a boat
Ghebguby, neck, chin, jaw
Ghemm, grief, trouble
Ghemzeh, a glance, wink
Ghùl, an imaginary monster
Ghuncheh, a bud, rose-bud
Ghurret, Aurora, dawn
Gueem, I may, say
Giriften, or *Gooriftun*, to take, seize
Goft, or *Guft*, he said, spoke
Goftend, they said, &c.
Gohur, a gem, a jewel
Gudeshtun, or *Guzashtun*, to pass by
Guftar, a speech, a word
Gùl, a rose, a flower
Gulaub, rosewater
Gulazaur, rosy cheeked
Gulendaum, rosy hue
Gulshen, a rose garden
Gulzar, a bed of roses
Gumariden, to compel, to gnash the teeth, &c.
Gumaun, a doubt, opinion
Gunge, a treasure
Gurdaniden, to cause to be done
Guzeshtun, to pass by, or near
Guzaf, vanity, an idle foolish saying

H.

Hail, terrible, dreadful, horrible
Haram, forbidden
Hasyl, gain, result, advantage
Haul, condition, time, present
Hedees or *Hedys*, news, story, &c.
Heech, none, no, never, not at all
Hekayet, story, narration
Hekyket, truth, reality
Hem, together, with
Hemchu, like, as
Hemchunaun, thus, in this manner
Hemchunaunk, in like manner as
Hemeh, or *hemè*, all, every
Hemidoon, so, in like manner, always
Hem Kauneh, of the same house living together
Hemrah, a companion
Hemzad, born together, partners
Hena, or *Huna*, here, this place
Her, every, all, both
Her doo, both the one and the other
Hereer, silken stuff
Heyhat, a desart
Hezret, majesty, dignity
Hind, India, Hindoostan
Hoosh, understanding, sense, reason
Houri, a virgin of paradise
Huna, see *Hena*

VOCABULARY.

Huftum, the eighth
Huwa, the air

I.

Ikaub, an eagle
Illa, unless, but,
Imrooz, to day, this day,
Imſheb, this night
Infaun, a man, human creature
Iràk, Chaldea
Irem, a fabulous garden of delight
Iſhaun, they, them, &c.
Iſtigfaur, repentance, aſking pardon
Iſhk or *Yſhk*, violent love
Iſtikbaul, futurity meeting, &c.
Iſm, a name
Izaur, the cheek, face, &c.

J.

Janeb, the ſide, part
Javab, an anſwer
Jauée, a place
Jaum, a goblet, cup
Jaun, the ſoul, life
Jaunaun, lovely woman, miſtreſs
Jaunet, thy ſoul
Jauvedaun, eternal, perpetual
Jawy, a ſtream, river
Jemaul, beauty, elegance
Jemd, armies, troops
Jeraud, the locuſt

Jung, war, battle, fight
Junoon, madneſs, inſanity
Juvauny, youth
Juz, except, but, &c.

K.

Kaum, wiſh, deſire, &c.
Kamus, the ocean, title of a celebrated Arabic Dictionary, tranſlated and publiſhed by Golius
Kar, work, buſineſs, labour
Kaſhgy, would to heaven
Ked, ſtature
Kee or *Ky*, who
Keh, who, how, which, for, becauſe that
Keiſooy, locks, ringlets
Kemaun, a bow
Kemer, waiſt
Keneezy, a girl, a damſel
Kerar, firmneſs, tranquillity
Kerm, generoſity, humane
Keryet, a city or town
Keſterauiden, to cauſe to be ſpread as a carpet or couch
Keſterd, ſpread
Kes, ſome one, any one, a perſon
Keſhud, ſhe opened
Keſimet, ſhare, portion
Khaneh, a houſe
Kevſar, Ceſar, a monarch

VOCABULARY.

Khan, an inn, family, a table
Khatemáko, their feals, Arab
Khar, a thorn
Khara, a hard ftone
Khater, difpofition, inclination
Khaub, a bed, fleep, dream
Khaukh, earth, clay
Khauhed, 3d p. fing. from
Khauften, to afk, wifh, defire
Kheez, arife thou
Khendaun, fmiling, charming
Kheyaul, fancy, imagination
Khoob, fair, beautiful, good
Khoobaun, plural of *Khoob*
Khood, felf, ones own
Khoon, blood
Khoord, eats
Khoorm, delightful, pleafant
Khoofh, fweet, pleafant
Khoofh Ku, or *Kaw*, a fweet finger
Khorfheed, the fun
Khofhnud, appeafed, fatisfied
Khulayek, the fame as
Khulky, the people, inhabitants
Khruydmund, wife, learned, prudent
Khufby, thou flumbereft
Khuzaun, autumn, the fall of the leaf
Kohen, old, ancient
Kol, every, all
Kuja, where, wherefoever

Kulaum, words, difcourfe, fpeech
Kumbed, a vault, arch, tower, &c.
Kumend, fnare, noofe
Kumr, full moon
Kunar, a brim, border, embrace, &c.
Kuni, thou doeft
Kurdeh, done, participle
Kufar, a palace, &c.
Kufhad, gladnefs, rejoicing
Kufhayy, thou openeft, loofeft, &c.
Kufhteh, killed
Kufhtend, they became, &c.
Kût, food, nourifhment

L.

La, not, no, &c.
Laabet, a charmer, alluring by beauty
Laleh, a tulip
Lafhkur, an army
Leb, the lip
Leiken, but
Leka, face, form, &c.

M.

Mah, the moon
Mah-e-peikur, fair-faced as the moon
Mahy, a fifh
Mandeh, remained

VOCABULARY.

Many, thou remainest, also the name of a famous painter
Maun, a family estate
Maunend, like, resembling
Mebad, let there not be
Me ber, do not bear, support
Meh-roo, Moon-faced, lovely
Mehejur, cut off, forsaken, separated
Meï, wine
Mehunnet, affliction, calamity
Mekaum, place, station
Mekuddem, preceding, before, &c.
Melal, grief, vexation
Mellek, the Locust
Memkin, possible
Memkin Nebuved, could not possibly be
Men, (Pers:) I, me, mine
Men or *Min*, (Arab:) from, than
Menzil, a mansion, residence
Meshryk, the East
Mesr, Egypt, Cairo
Mezkan, eye lashes
Mihr, the Sun, a seal
Mikend, he acts the part of, does, they do, make, &c.
Mikeshy, thou loosest, dishevelest
Mikezeshet, or *Miguzesht*, passes by
Mikhauft, intreats, wishes for
Mikhoory, thou drinkest

Minar, *Minaur*, a turret, column
Mijk or *Mijk'on*, (Arab:) musk
Miroom, I go, I am going
Misl, equal to, like
Mizend, *(Nubet,)* he sets the watch, &c.
Moonis, companion
Mooee, locks, hair, ringlets
Mubaruck, happy, prosperous
Mugur, perhaps, unless
Muhammed, Mahomet
Muheyia, prepared, arranged
Mulluk, an angel
Murd, a man
Mushkeen, musky
Mushtak, longing for, desirous
Musk, musk
Musnud, the throne
Mutrib, a minstrel, musician

N.

Na, negative, particle, prefixed, as, in
Na-aumeed, hopeless, not hoping,
Naim, gift, blessing
Nakhasht, picture, painter, &c.
Nam, or *Naum*, a name
Nameh, a book, letter, history
Nauleh, lamentation, murmurs, plaintive notes
Nauruz, or *Nurooz*, first day of Spring

VOCABULARY.

Nazrauny, a Christian
Nazuk, graceful, lovely
Nazuneen, graceful, elegant
Nebuved, was not
Neda, exclamation, clamour
Nedarem, I hold not, &c.
Nedaunem, I know not
Nedeedeh, not seen
Neerung, charms, spels
Negahy, look, glance
Nehaden, to place
Nehen, A. we
Neh, not, also, place thou
Nehy, you may place
Nekhauhem, I do not wish, ask
Nekhauhed, does not wish, ask
Nekhet, smell, perfume
Nekuned, they do not, make not,
Neshayed, it is not meet, fit
Nesheeneed, he heard not
Nesret, splendor, beauty
Niayed, does not come, go
Nimet, benefits, blessings
Niseem, a gale, breeze
Nisheshun, to fit
Nishki, Arabic, hand-writing
Noah, a proper name
Noorooz, the first day of Spring
Nubehaur, the New Year, Spring
Nubet, a turn, time, watch
Nughmet, melody, music
Nukkul, tradition, narration

Numoodun, to show
Nutvaun, it is impossible, cannot
Nuzim, verses, poetry.

O.

O, or *Oee*, he, she, it, his, &c.
Ora, to him, her, &c, him, it, &c. her
Organoon, a musical instrument
Ottar, essence, perfume

P.

Pa, or *Pauee*, the foot
Padir, father
Padishah, or *Padishaw*, a king
Pahlavi, the ancient language of Persia
Pakeezeh, fair, pure, lovely
Paureh, or *Pareh*, a bit, piece, part
Pechegaun, infants, children
Pedrudy Kirdun, to bid farewell
Peer, old, an old man
Peery, old age
Peikur, the face, form, &c.
Peish, before
Pend, counsel, advice
Pereeden, to fly in the air
Perdeh, or *Pordeh*, a curtain, veil, hangings
Pery, a fairy, angel
Pes, after, then

VOCABULARY.

Pefy, many, more, &c.
Picheeden, to twift, bend, involve
Pidaw, openly, manifeftly, &c.
Pihen, wide, ample
Por, full
Pordehdary, a chamberlain, or holder of the curtain
Pufheedeh, clothed, covered

R.

Raheem, merciful, compaffionate
Rahman, merciful
Raoud, or *Rouz*, a garden
Reehaun, fragrant herbs
Reekfend, they dance, leap
Reez, pour out
Refy, benediction, bleffing
Refed, comes to
Rift, went, departed
Rifk, envy
Rood, or *Rùd*, a river, ftring of a mufical inftrument
Rooee, the face
Roomiaun, the Grecians, Europeans
Ruah, a fpirit, breath
Rud, a river, ftring of a mufical inftrument, he goes
Ruhmet, mercy, compaffion
Rung, colours, complexion
Rufhenay, fplendor, light
Rufool, prophet, ambaffador

Ruvàn, running, flowing
Ryaheen, odoriferous herbs

S.

Saaty, a while, fpace of time
Sabr, patience
Sad, an hundred
Sádi, or *Saadi*, a poet's name
Sagher, a cup, goblet
Salam, falutation, peace, fafety
Sauktun, to do, make, prepare
Sauky, a cup bearer, water-carrier
Sauny, fecond
Sauz, any mufical inftrument
Sazee, thou makeft
Seba, zephyr
See, thirty
Seemeen, filvery, made of filver,
Seemten, filver-bodied
Seh, or *Suh*, three
Sehn, a court-yard, a fquare
Sehra, a defart
Sehrauny, defarts
Sekhun, difcourfe, words, &c.
Selfebeel, a celeftial fountain
Seneman, idols
Sepeed, white
Ser, the head, top, extremity, &c.
Seranjaum, end, conclufion
Serifhteh, compounded, formed
Seyah, black
Sikander, **Alexander**

VOCABULARY.

Shady, gladnefs, joy
Shah, or *Shaw*, a king
Shaar, poetry, verfe
Shah-var, royal, belonging to, or like a king
Shaikh, an elder, a chief
Shawk, a tender branch
Sheb, night
Sheh, for *Shah*, a king
Shehed, honey
Sheher, a city
Shekhefteh, broken
Shekur, fugar
Shemáa, a candle, taper, &c.
Sheneeden, to hear
Sheraub, wine, fherbet, liquor
Shimfhad, the box tree
Shirauz, a famous city
Shireen, fweet, pleafant
Shraub, wine, liquor
Shud, was, he, fhe, it was, &c.
Shudun, to be
Shuky, mirth, jollity
Sooee, towards
Sooz, burning, tormenting
Suim, the third
Sultaun, prince, fultan
Sulub, plundered, deftroyed
Suluh, peace, concord
Suw-waur, horfeman, riding

T.

Ta, that, until, in order that
Tabaun, bright, fhining
Takht, a throne
Tályk, hanging, the Perfian hand writing
Tawk, power, ftrength
Teer, an arrow, the Tigris
Temafha, fhow, entertainment
Temaum, intire, whole, complete
Ten, the body
Tenha, alone
Tenk, narrow, barren
Tera, oblique cafe of *too*, thou
Teftym, faluting, granting
Too or *tù*, thou, you, thine
Toocheh, turning, converfion
Tubaà, nature, genius, difpofition
Tulby, thou feekeft, from
Tulbeedun, to feek
Tulb Kirdun, to feek
Turkaun, turks, beautiful perfons
Turreh, ringlets, locks, &c.

V. U.

Va, *Vaw*, *Ve*, *Waw*, *U*, and *Var*, added to nouns, denotes fimilitude, as *Peri-var*, like a fairy
Vely, but
Ulfety, familiarity, fociety
Umr, life

VOCABULARY.

W.

Walid, parent, progenitor
Wallah, by GOD! oh GOD!
Waw, the copulative *and*
Wazia, eftablifhing, legiflating
Wehifet, a difh of locufts
Wehifhet, affliction
Wekt, feafon, time
Wekta, once upon a time

Y.

Ya Arab: oh! ho!
Ya, Pers: or
Yabed, may find, from
Yaften, to find
Yar, a friend, a miftrefs
Yehoody, a Jew
Yek-fheby, one night
Yeky, one, a fingle one
Yeminy, belonging to Arabia, Felix
Yfh, mirth, joy
Yunaniaun, Ionians, Greeks

Z.

Zawiyet, hermitage, cell-cloyfter
Ze, for *Az*, from, of, &c.
Zeeba, elegant, graceful, &c.
Zeer, under
Zemeen, ground, country, land
Zendaun, a prifon
Zendeh-am, I am alive
Zendegy, exiftence, life
Zehreh, Venus
Zoormund, powerful, ftrong
Zubanny, tongue
Zulf, a ringlet, lock of hair
Zunjeer, a chain, fetter
Zun, a woman
Zun, a ftriker, player on, as *Organoon Zun*, a player on the organ
Zufht, deformed, hideous, unpleafant, ugly, &c.
Zuwal, declenfion, fetting of the fun

GENERAL

GENERAL TABLE

OF

CONTENTS.

               PAGE
ADONIS, ...183, 184
Afrafiab, Introd,..............xiv.
Ahafuerus, ... 98
Ahu, or fawn................127
Alcoran, fee " Koran"
Alexander, Introd. xi. 52, 74, 75, 96,
               116, 131, 133
Allegory, Introd. ... .xx. xxxii
Amorous, fee " Erotick"
Anacreon, Introd.xxiii.xxx, 125, 149,
              152, 158
Ancient Poetry, Introd.........xix.
Angels,.............87, 135, 137
Antiques found, Introd. ....xvi.
Anvari, (the poet).......19, 21, 125
Arabia, temple difcovered in the defarts
   of, Introd.................xvi
Arabian mufic, ...160

               PAGE
Arabian Saints,..........166, 172
——— Writers, inacurate......84
Araxes (River)..............101
Ariofto, ...139
Ariftophanes, ...132
Armenia, ...102
Artaxerxes, ...98
Afp. (the word) a common termina-
   nation of proper names,......14

BABYLON, Introd. xvii, 104, 105,
             106, 109
Bacchanalian, Introd........xx, 18
Balkh, ...99
Barbary, ...31, 32, 176
Beauty, 26, 86, 87, 110, 113, 123,
   126, 134, 137, 138, 140, 150
             151, 179
Beharistàn, ...17

TABLE OF CONTENTS.

	PAGE
Benediction, (Perfian)	140, 142
Black Eyes,	123, 124, 127, 187
Bokhara,	49, 101
Bulbul, fee " Nightingale"	
CAF, a fabulous mountain,	54
Cairo,	107
Canaan,	184
Cafhmere,	162
———— writer of,	115
———— Nymphs of,	123
———— Singing Women of,	162
Cafpian Sea,	101
Caflem, (the poet)	21
Caftle of the white giant,	98
Chaldaick, Introd. xxx, 105, 106, 109, 110, 117
Chehelminar, (fee Perfepolis)	
Cherub	137
Combat of Ruftam, with the Deeve Sepeed,	93, 97
———— with Sohraub,	115
Conclufion of Arabic and Perfian MSS. like the early printed books in Europe	71
Conftantinople, Introd.	xiv
Creed, (Mahometan)	177
Cufa, or Chaldea,	99, 105
Cufick,	188
Cuthites,	109
Cyrus, Introd.	xv
DARIUS, 3, 23, 79, 16. Introd. xiv.
Dates, according to Mahometan æra 88
Dæmon, (See Deeve)	

	PAGE
Deeve or Dive,	92, 95, 98, 136
——— Sepeed, or white giant,	98
Dejleh (river Tigris)	99, 102, 103, 108
Deri,	1
Devil, (names of)	96
Devotion,	19
Diana's temple at Perfepolis, Introd. xvii.
Dictionary (Perfian) Introd.	xxvi
ECHO, "the daughter of Voice"	156
Egypt, 83, 107, 109, 183, 184, 188
Elegiac, Introd.	xx, 20
Elegy,	76, 185
Enthufiafm, in Devotion and Love	18
Epitaph of Sir Wm Jones,	185
Epithets,	122, 123, 125, 155
Erotick, Introd.	xxi, 13
Errors in MSS.	6, 7, 9
Eulogium on Sir Wm. Jones,	184
Euphrates, fee " Fràt,"	
Eufoofy (Infhai)	141
FAIRY, fee " Pery,"	
——— vifion of Milton	139
Ferdufi, or Firdaufi, 78, 81, 94, 95, 97, 112, 115. Introd. xxiii.
Frat or Furàt, the river Euphrates,	99, 104, 105, 109
GABRIELLE DE VERGY,	146
Ganges, (River)	107, 110
Ghùl, (a Dæmon)	96
Giant, (the white)	98
Gihoon, (river Oxus)	49, 99, 100, 101

TABLE OF CONTENTS.

GOD, name in Perfian, Arabic, Affyrian, ancient language of the Guebres, &c.......... 34
Greek and Perfian poetry, compared Introd........... xxii. xxiii.
——— Dialects 118
——— Muficians, ... 130
——— Mufic, ... 160
——— Scribes, ... 39
——— Writings, ---75, 78, 103, 117
——— Tranflations of Perfian manufcripts, Introd. xi.
Gumaun, ... 49

HAFIZ, or Hafez, 21, 28, 49, 76, 119, 123, 152, 160, 163, 184, 185, Introd. xxiii.
Hebrew, 14, 30, 44, 65, 78, 96, 105 Introd. xxx. 106, 108, 117, 118, 133, 137
Herkern, (Infhai) 141
Hindooftan, ... 4, 6, 101
Horfe, (fee Afp)
Houries, ... 62, 87, 124, 137, 187

JAMI, (the Poet) 17, 18, 20, 21, 82, 83, 88, 104, 119, 136, 163, 183, 185, 187, 189
Jaun and Jaunaun, play on the words, 164
Impurities, ... 19, 58
Indelicate Verfes, ... 19
India, ... 5, 6, 106

Indian Munfhies, ... 6
——— Mufic 160
Indus River, ... 101
Infcriptions, Perfepolitan. ... 2, 4, 98
——— Cufic, ... 88
Inftruments of Mufic, .130, 160, 161
Johannes Secundus, ... 145
Jones, Sir William, ... 184
Ionians, (Greeks) 132
Jofeph, 16, 18, 67, 82, 182, 184, 185, 187, &c.
Iràk, or Chaldea, ... 103, 167, 176
Iraun, or Perfia, ... 6, 101, 115
Irem, (the Garden of) 65
Ifaphàn, (City of) 27, 28
Italian, like Perfian, Introd. xxi
——— Cuftoms, like Perfian, Introd. xxii
Ivy, ... 142

KARE, (or Ciaro) 107
Kemalleddin, (the Poet)........ 28
Kahcani, (the Poet) 103
Khofroo, (the Poet) 21, 120
Kifs, ... 152, 153, 156
Kifs of Venus, ... 145
Koran, 1, 56, 65, 69, 74, 81, 106, 120, 124, 128, 129, 182, 183, 189
Kumaun, ... 49

LEGENDS, ... 177
Letter-writing, ... 141
Library, Introd. .... xxii. 12

TABLE OF CONTENTS.

Locusts, ... 166, 174, 175
Love, Introd. xxxi, 18, 19, 20, 82, 83,
    114, 146, 152, 161, 163, 179,
    182, 186
Luxuries, transpainted into Greece, 128
——— of Shiraz, ... 27
——— Persian 151, 153
Lybia, ... 176
Lyric, Introd. xxiii, 19, 21, 148, 184

MAGIC, Introd. ...... xiii. xx, 106
Mahomet, see Mohammed
Mahometan Creed, ... 177
——— Saints, ... 166, 173
Man, in a general and particular
    sense, ... 35
Mani, the painter and Heresiarch, 51,
    52
Mausolea at Persepolis, Introd. xviii
Medes, ... 104
Messiah, ... 88
Miracles, ... 166, 174, 177
Miraculous Anecdote, ... 166
Mohammed, or Mahomet, 1, 81, 183,
    189
Moors of Barbary, or Western Arabs,
    31, 32, 176
Mosellay, (the Bower of) 28
Moses, ... 183, 189
Munshies, (or Moonshies) 6
Music, Introd. xx. xxxi, 113, 130,
    131, 132, 133, 150, 151, 152,
    160

Musk, ... 62, 122, 127, 128

NADIR SHAH 9
Nakhshebi, ... 161
Nameh, (Mughenny) or address to the
    Musician, ... 160
Nameh, (Shah) or Book of Kings,
    Introd. xxxi, 80, 94, 97, 112
Nameh, (Skander) or History of
    See Alexander, Introd. xxxi
Nameh, (Tooti) or Tales of a Parrot,
    161
Nasser ben Hareth, ... 81
Nezami, (the Poet) Introd. xi, 7,
    23, 51, 52, 75, 76, 77, 79,
    96, 131, 160
Nightingale, 48, 88, 91, 143, 145,
    147, 157, 158, Introd. xxx. xxxii
Nile, ... 107, 108, 109
Nizami, see Nezami
Noah, ... 56
Numerical Figures, ... 70, 87
Nymphs of Cashmere, ... 123

ODE by Jami, ... 20
Organ 140, 132

PAHLAVI, or Pehlavi, 3, 106, 133,
    Introd. xi, xix
Painting, Introd. xii, 6, 10, 51, 52, 97
Palace, Introd. .... xiii, xv, 114
Paradise, 62, 65, 99, 101, 107, 108, 110,
    118, 124, 128, 186, 187

5

TABLE OF CONTENTS.

Parrot, (Tales of a) 161
Pehlavi, ...3, 106, 133
Perfumes, 62, 113, 127, 128, 129, 138, Introd. xxx.
Peries, 62, 86, 95, 134, 138, 140, Introd. xxx
Persepolis, 2, 3. 98, 114, Introd. xv.
Persepolitan Inscriptions, ...2, 4, 98,
Persia, or Iraun, ...6, 101, 115
Persian Literature, styled "soft and "elegant," Introd. xxi
Pery, see Peries,
Petrarch, Introd...........xxi, 158
Philip of Macedon, ...79, 131
Piety, ...19
Plato, ...132
Pomp of Persian Kings, Introd...xiii.
Potiphar, ...182
Price of Manuscripts,.........8, 9
Princess of Sitemgan, Introd. xvii, 113
Pronunciation of Eastern Words, Introd. xxvii

RAIL,....................182
Raoul de Coucy, ...146
Religious,..................18
Rivers, held in veneration,......109
River Araxes, ...101
—— Euphrates, ... 99, 104, 109
—— Gihon, ...100, 102
—— Ganges,............107, 110
—— Iaxartes,...............102
—— Indus,..................101
—— Nile,.........107, 108, 109

River Oxus, ...100, 102
—— Sihoon,............102, 104
—— Tigris,.....99, 102, 103, 108
Roknabad, ...28
Romance of the four Dervishes, 126, 127
Romances, Introd. xxxii. 54, 80, 81, 82, 98, 126
Rose, called "the flower," per excellentiam, ...33
Rose water,..................42
Roses, (Ottar of) 42, 26, 88, 91, 125, 127, 129, 143, 145, 157, 158, Introd. xxxi.
Roxana,....................117
Rustam, the Persian Hero, Introd. xvii. 80, 81, 92, 93, 96, 97, 110, 112, 114

SADI, (the poet) Introd. xxxii, 19, 21, 28, 54, 56, 57, 58
—— his portrait,............59
—— works, 85, 86, 91, 103, 119, 144, 148, 155, 158
Saints,..................166, 173
Samarcand,..................123
Sanscrit,................109, 184
Sawky (or cup-bearer). 119, 150, 153, 159, Introd. xxxi
Science, Introd............. xxxi
Scythia or Touràn,....101 113, 115
Selsebeel, (a fountain).........118
Senai (the Poet) 21, 163
Seraph, ...137

E e

TABLE OF CONTENTS.

	PAGE
Shah Caſſem Anver (the Poet)	151
Shah Nameh,	80, 94, 97, 112
Shaikh,	173
Shirauz,	26, 28, 56, 59, 97, 98, 120, 123, 147
Simurgh, a fabulous animal,	54
Singing women,	153
Sitemgan,	133
Skander, (fee Alexander)	
Sohraub,	80, 115
Sonnet of Jami,	20
Sonnets of Petrarch, Introd.	xxi
Spring, Introd. xxxi,	91, 143, 157, 158, 159, 185
Studious (the Perſians)	7
Sun,	33, 46
TALES of a Parrot,	161
Tapeſtry,	113
Temple diſcovered in the deſart of Arabia, Introd.	xvi
Temple of Diana, Introd.	xvii
Tooti Nameh, or " Tales of a Parrot,"	161

	PAGE
Touraun or Scythia,	101, 113, 115
Turkiſh writer	183
VENUS,	125, 126, 145, 152, 187
Venus's Kiſs,	145
WESTERN Arabs,	31, 37, 176
Wine, Introd. xxxi.	26, 113, 118, 119, 120, 129, 150, 151, 152, 153, 155, 156
Women, beautiful at Shirauz,	26
—— Dancing,	153
—— Singing,	153, 162
YAFEI AL YEMINI, an Arabian writer,	172, 177
ZELEEKHA,	16, 18, 67, 82, 179
Zend,	3, 4, 37
Zendaveſta,	37
Zeratuſht, Zerdehuſht, Zoroaſter,	3, 25, 37

FINIS.

THE
PLATES

ARE TO BE PLACED IN THE FOLLOWING ORDER:

Frontispiece

Plate I.   To face Page 11.
— II.   ——— 23.
— III.   ——— 45.
— IV.   ——— 53.
— V.   ——— 73.
— VI.   ——— 92.
— VII.   ——— 116.
— VIII.   ——— 143.
— IX.   ——— 165.

ERRATA.

Page xxi Introduction, Note, for *ille*, read *illæ*.
—— 20 Line 4, for *ſtyel*, read *ſtyle*.
—— 35 —— the laſt, for דם read אדם
—— 88 —— 22, for *Padua*, read *Pavia*.
—— 157 —— 16, for *amantuim*, read *amantium*.
—— 185 —— 20, for *fecudus*, read *fecundus*.
—— 186 —— 3, for *Bulu*, read *Bulee*.
—— ib. —— ib. for *behiſht*, read *behiſht*.

IN THE VOCABULARY, INSERT

Muhur, the ſun, a ſtamp, impreſſion.——And, *Mikhendend*, they ſmile, laugh, &c.

www.ingramcontent.com/pod-product-compliance
Lightning Source LLC
Chambersburg PA
CBHW032136230426
43672CB00011B/2351